UNSEEN WOUNDS OF WOMEN

CAROLINE STRAWSON

Disclaimer

In parts throughout this book, the co-authors may describe events, locales and conversations from their memories. Sometimes, in order to maintain their anonymity, in some instances we have changed the names of individuals and places, we may have changed some identifying characteristics and details such as physical properties, occupations and places of residence.

Although the co-authors and publisher have made every effort to ensure that the information in this book was correct at press time, the co-authors and publisher do not assume and hereby disclaim any liability to any party for any loss, damage, or disruption caused by errors or omissions, whether such errors or omissions result from negligence, accident, or any other cause.

Copyright © 2022 by Caroline Strawson

ISBN13 Paperback: 979-8-847827-79-9

All rights reserved.

No part of this book may be reproduced in any form or by any electronic or mechanical means, including information storage and retrieval systems, without written permission from the authors, except for the use of brief quotations in a book review.

CONTENTS

1. MY INVISIBLE CAGE   5
Caroline Strawson

About the Author   25

2. NOT THAT WOMAN ANYMORE   27
Andrea Elizabeth

About the Author   41

3. UNSEEN MOTHER WOUND   43
Brooke Bownes

About the Author   58

4. INTERNAL CONFLICT WOUNDS™   60
Christa Cusack O'Neill

About the Author   80

5. LOST AND FOUND   82
Gaby Engelbrecht

About the Author   101

6. I FEEL LIKE I CAN BREATHE AGAIN!   103
Heather Black

About the Author   119

7. ASSAULT OF THE HEART   121
Houa Utech

About the Author   137

8. LATHER, RINSE, REPEAT... UNTIL YOU DON'T.   139
Jessica Parente

About the Author   156

9. THE GIRL FROM THE WRONG SIDE OF THE RIVER   158
Joanne Fisher

About the Author   175

10. THE SILENT SCREAMS WITHIN 177
Kim Pontarelli

About the Author 196

11. THE SKIN I'M IN 198
Lesley Lee

About the Author 217

12. THE REJECTION WOUND : HOW TO HEAL
AND SET YOURSELF FREE 219
Noshiela Maqsood

About the Author 236

13. UNCONDITIONAL 238
Rayna Pattee Isaacson

About the Author 256

14. RELEASING PAIN TO FIND PEACE: A
WELLNESS JOURNEY 258
Rebecca Mitchell

About the Author 272

15. FEEDING THE WOLF 274
Valerie Sussman, MD.

About the Author 287

1

MY INVISIBLE CAGE

CAROLINE STRAWSON

I STILL HAVE TO PINCH MYSELF AS TO WHERE MY LIFE IS NOW. The fact that each day I get to help thousands of women globally deeply heal from trauma, such as domestic and narcissistic abuse. That through my own darkness, I can now be that ray of light at the end of, what can seem like, a long, dark tunnel. Through my own deep inner healing journey interwoven with my skillset around being a trauma informed positive psychology coach and somatic therapist helping others to move from post-traumatic stress to post traumatic growth.

Post traumatic growth is a positive psychology term that literally means that you find your purpose and strength from your own pain and struggle and can actually go on to lead an even more joyful, purposeful and deeply connected life because of the trauma you have experienced. I know that may seem impossible to you even right now, but I have helped and supported thousands of women to experience post traumatic growth and could not be prouder of them.

When I was in deep pain and feeling so much shame after my divorce from a narcissist, I now know that my darkness of losing everything including my family home and being in over $100,000 debt suffering with complex PTSD, depression, anxiety, self-harm and panic attacks enabled me to literally hit rock bottom and to find my true purpose in this deep pain and enabling me now to be completely debt free and totally financially independent to buying a $750,000 home in June 2021 in my own name, solely supporting my children to be privately educated, building my Accredited School of Embodied Trauma Informed Living toa seven figure international therapy and coaching business focused on helping women thrive after trauma and abuse, teaching others how to do the work I now do plus training and consulting in the corporate world so that we create a global ripple effect of healing, compassion and kindness and break this generational cycle of trauma. I start each day filled with gratitude for the joy and deep connection I now feel in my life.

One of the biggest gifts of this growth has been watching my children turn into the most confident and compassionate human beings. They understand human behavior to a level that I only began to in my forties! They totally see that others people's behavior is never a reflection of them but merely a projection of the other person's pain on to them.

I am in awe of them but know that this is only because I took my own healing so seriously. It may have taken me a few years to do this, but better late than never! I have been their role model and I have given them the gift of self-love so that they will never find themselves in relationships like I had because they know boundaries, red flags and know what they deserve. When you heal yourself, you really do heal the next generation.

Imagine a world like this... this is my drive and why I am so passionate about the work that I do but it was not always like that.

I used to feel like I was living in this invisible cage. A cage with that was driven by society, parenting, marriage, career, relationships! Basically, everyone and everything else but me.

I was trapped in this cage of conformity driven by having to live my life from the expectations of others. How did they need me to act, behave, look and be to keep everyone else happy? Damn those Disney fairy tales of meet your Prince Charming and live happily ever! These have haunted me all of my life because this was what life was supposed to be? That if you were sad, hurt or unable to protect yourself, a man would come and rescue you and then all would be good in the world, and you would be looked after forever and made to feel safe and protected from the man in your life? That this is what is meant to happen if we go by the books I was brought up on.

I had grown up with the deep understanding that my role on this planet was to please others. I am not blaming my parents because let's face it, parenting does not come with a manual...if only! My parents were always doing the best that they could with how they were parented and whilst my mother wanted myself and my two older sisters to get university degrees, there was always an element of glass ceiling as we were women and women grew up, got married, had children and lived a life creating a home and the husband was the one who was the provider. My mother stayed at home and my dad went out to work. I had been conditioned into a role of pleasing others and needing to hit certain expectations especially around academics. This was what my parents saw as them doing a good job. If I got *As* at school, that was what was expected and made them feel like they were doing what they needed to do and a good job as a parent. It was what was expected.

This haunted me for years because my relationship with my father was one of constant needing to feel like I was pleasing him and seeking out his approval and academics was just one of the ways I would try to gain approval and get praise from him. Academics seemed to be his version of love, or so I interpreted. But the praise never came. I would bring reports home that were excellent in the desperate hope my father would tell me how proud he was, but it never came.

My interpretation of this as a child was that I needed to try harder and that what I was doing then must not be good enough. I needed to do more and more in the hope that surely that would then be enough, and I would get the *'Well done, I am so proud of you'* that I desperately sought? But it never came. My mother on the other hand was the complete opposite! She needed me to be happy with her so that she knew what a great mother she was. Food was very much one of her ways of showing love! I learnt to associate food with love and even today if I feel like I don't matter, I must be mindful not to reach for a bag of crisps or a packet of biscuits to give myself that feeling of love that I got from my childhood with food from my mother, especially as she passed away in 2009.

No surprise that as an adult I was a people pleasing, perfectionist, high achieving, emotional eater. Even as an adult I could look back and see that of course I was good enough just for being me, but my body was telling a different story because my actions did not match my thoughts. This is exactly why I trained in somatic and embodiment coaching and therapy because I realized that no matter what we think, if we don't work deep in the body at a nervous system level, we will always react from our wounded inner child, even if we are now an adult.

I realized that all the reading, watching videos, listening to podcasts and having counselling and talk therapy had all helped because it had helped validate my experiences in a narcissistic marriage, but I still felt like each day, my emotions would still get the better of me. I knew I was good enough but every time someone said something where I thought they hadn't listened or feel like they did not believe me, I would get upset, hurt and angry and this would flood my body with emotions.

This was when I researched and realized that I was missing a huge piece in my trauma healing which was the body work. I needed to process past emotional trauma and timestamp it into the past so that my body could remember and not keep reliving the pain as if it was still happening in the present. I realized that I knew all about certain aspects of my body such as periods and reproductive system and even bones and muscles form my science degree, but I had never been taught about my nervous system and why we feel the way we do. It has been truly a transformative process both in my own healing and now retraining and helping and educating others to do the same. I realized that the key to my invisible cage was held in my own body and healing the deep inner child wounds that I had to unlock it myself and not get others to do it for me.

As the youngest of three daughters, this really shaped me with my relationship with my parents. When we are born as children, we come into the world wired for love and connection. Then our childhood experiences and the key part, our interpretation of these experiences and people and events around us, really shape the types of inner wounds we start to create around what we think and feel about ourselves. I always thought I had grown up with a great childhood and that is not to say that I didn't, but I think I was twenty-three years old before I realized my parents were human beings. This may seem ridiculous, but I thought they were always right, what they said was always the truth and the right thing and that they never made mistakes.

When I was growing up, my middle sister had a hole in her heart. She was born with this, and it was corrected when she was eleven with open heart surgery. Now as adults within our family, we knew the stories of this and understood how hard this must have been for my sister and of course my parents, but what I never realized was that it was events like this that really shaped my beliefs about myself as a child. Naturally my parents treated my sister in a certain way due to the worry and knowledge of her heart condition and they were so good at ensuring that my sister was cared for and shown how brave and invincible she was. Rightly so, as that is what any parent would do. But actually, this had a huge impact on me as the youngest. What about me? Why wasn't I getting all this attention? Was I not good enough? Did I not matter enough to get this attention?

Of course, as an adult now and looking back, I could completely understand why my parents acted in the way that they did, but that was not my interpretation of this as a child. My perception was that I was not good enough, I felt invisible and not important enough to get that amount attention and type of love. A child's logic.

This is why we feel we are judged so much as adults because we can see when we look back at the story that it was not us, but our body and nervous system is telling a different story because that pain got wired into me as a child and no amount of affirmations or talking can change that. It has to be the body work.

As a child, I started to be louder, make people laugh and perform little shows with impressions trying to be seen and heard. Desperately looking for approval and love. This gave me some attention as everyone would watch and laugh but it still didn't feel quite enough. I would then be really, really, really good at school and I mean a role model student. I would get everyone to like me including the teachers because I was driven by proving my worth. I would play sport with such drive that I became captain of teams and playing at a higher level of sport. I felt so compelled that I needed to show everyone that I was good enough, that I was important, and I was worthy.

It was exhausting!

It is no surprise to me now as I look back that from the age of about six, I started to suffer badly with tonsillitis. To the extent that I was off school almost monthly for a few days and whilst I hated missing school as I did not want anyone to think badly of me. I got so much attention from my mother that it was like a dream for me. This became a pattern until I was eleven years old when I then had my tonsils out. I am convinced to this day, that I created tonsillitis as a part of me to receive love to feel good enough. I became so co-dependent on my mother to show me my sense of worth because I really did not feel that from my father. My dad was not an emotional man so would never praise me and whilst he worked hard, and drove me to sports events, I needed to hear the words from him, but they just never came.

Now again, as an adult I can see that this came from his own childhood because he grew up with parents who again, were doing the best they could but there was arguments and no nurture and warmth. It was all about academics and grades and that was the way my father gained worth as that was what his parents thought was important. Academics became his version of love. This very much transcended into how he parented myself and my sisters where academics were so important. This meant that I was completely driven by protector parts in my inner system and became this high achieving, perfectionist, people pleaser. I was desperate to prove my worth because clearly what I was doing was not enough.

I even remember my sisters calling me the *BL from LB* which stood for the *Bum Licker from Leighton Buzzard* which was where we lived for a while! In fact, we used to joke about this as I was such a *goody two shoes* and as adults with our family stories, we would reminisce about this and whilst I would laugh, my body would again be telling a different story. I needed to be the *Bum Licker* as I had to do no wrong and then do more because surely then my father would praise and show me that I was good enough?!

What fascinates me is that as adults, we tell all these stories to each other and even laugh. But it really does highlight why we must never judge anyone about their behavior because there is always a reason why and that will always be about our childhood and our own perceptions which can all still be very different, even in the same family.

As the youngest, I always felt like I was the baby. In fact, I would say, it was only into my forties when I really did my own inner trauma work that I felt like I was fellow adults with my sisters and not the baby. Being the baby was just always reinforced by actions such as my father putting me in bed with my mother from ages six to nine years old. My mum used to snore like a wild African boar that would challenge anyone so my dad would pick me up out of my bed each night and put me in bed with my mum which I have to say, I loved. It felt warm and nice and safe. My safest place was with my mother. But this really reinforced that I was the baby of the family and couldn't even sleep alone. I felt like I had such a good relationship with my mother but realize now it was very enmeshed as my mother's sense of worth came from being a mother, so this was just reinforcing my need to need her. That I needed her to be happy and have a healthy sense of self as opposed to being interdependent knowing that I was an individual in my own right.

We need to stop looking just at present behavior and focus on the actual why someone behaves as they do with what has happened to them in the past. My drive was literally trying to be loved, to be liked, to have no one ever say anything bad about me, to get the highest grades, be the best at sport and literally be the best person that I could possibly be and this was literally non-negotiable. I simply could not feel the pain of not feeling good enough as a seven-year-old little girl, so my inner system was driven to have all these protector parts show up to prove to everyone that I was surely enough because then I would be able to stop doing more and being more because where I was finally would be enough. But it never was... so I would just keep trying!

When I look back, I can remember feeling like I was on guard all of the time, listening to words people said, watching for body language to interpret in a way that maybe they did not like me. I just could not have anyone think badly of me because that would just reinforce those inner child wounds which then must be true then. I felt like I was literally living in an invisible cage that no one could see. From the outside I looked like this happy go lucky young girl but inside I felt like I was in a cage and my body was screaming out for people to see the real me and that the real me was good enough. But because I did not dare take that risk, I had to portray myself as this perfect, people pleasing, perfectionist in the hope no one would notice that the real me, the true Caroline, was in fact not good enough.

From the moment I woke up to the moment I went to bed, I was driven by my need to have my parents thinking I was amazing, the teachers thinking I was amazing and my friends thinking I was a nice person. Anything less that that meant that I was really not good enough and that just felt too big a pain for me to bear. I wanted to scream *'I am good enough just for being me!'* but because I felt like no one had ever shown me that, I did not dare take the risk. Love and likability were conditional on me behaving a certain way. In fact, I used to get a lot of attention for the way I looked but this felt dirty to me because academics was how I needed to show my worth especially to my father. This could not be looks because that would mean I was stupid and if I was stupid, my dad would love me even less! I played that down and tried to work even harder!

My Invisible Cage

I am absolutely not blaming my parents here because they always did the best, they could with the programming they had from childhood, but I now clearly see that their behaviors massively influenced how I saw myself which in turn hugely impacted my friendships and my relationships as I got older.

In fact, I was probably the best friend and girlfriend you could ever have had because I would give and give and give almost to the point of exhaustion and sadly this was always to the detriment of my own happiness. It did not matter if I was exhausted or unhappy as long as the person I was with was happy because if they were happy, my nervous system could at least be a bit calmer safe in the knowledge that I must be good enough then? I had an anxious attachment that had come from my childhood.

But being this perpetual people pleaser, or codependent, meant that I then attracted toxic people who were people that loved to take, take and take some more. This meant that I was a magnet for abusive relationships because abusers and toxic people just home in on people who will try and please them, I mean why wouldn't they?

It was no surprise that in 1999, I found myself marrying a covert narcissist. Hindsight is a wonderful thing, and I can remember on August 14th, 1999, looking out of the window down at my husband to be feeling this apprehension in my gut but knowing that everything was paid for, and all the guests were waiting downstairs. From my invisible cage I found my voice saying, *'I do'* but inside my body was screaming *'I don't'*.

I knew something was off, but I could not put my finger on it, and we had already had problems before we even got married where I was left feeling discarded and unloved but then he would come back and say all the right things to fill that hole in my soul so I would finally feel what I had so desperately wanted to feel all along, that I was in fact good enough. This, I now know, to be love bombing. In fact, just a few months after we met, he even got a tattoo with my name on! He was giving me exactly what I was craving, and little did I know that this was a typical tactic of a narcissist to hook me right in. Saying and acting exactly what I needed to hear and feel to think I had found my Prince Charming.

During our marriage, I always felt like something was not quite right, but I put that down to his childhood and I just wanted to rescue, fix and make it better so then of course that would also mean that I was good enough. I always used to think that he was not on this planet, that he lacked presence even to the extent that when I was pregnant with our son, I remember saying to him that he had to stay present when he was caring for our son as this was another human being we had to look after and if something happened to our son, he couldn't hide it, he would have to be honest and share as it could be serious! I was worried that he may drop him or something and just not tell me.

Again, a massive red flag that I was even thinking this but I pushed this to one side because I had this drive to make the marriage work.

As time progressed and we had our son, my husband was a way a lot as he was cabin crew for an airline, so it felt like I was a single parent already and being highly codependent, I definitely got my sense of worth from being a mother.

The cycle continued. I had given my job up when we had our son even though I was in a higher position and earning more

My Invisible Cage

money, but again little did I know that this was just part of a narcissists tactic so that I was reliant on him not only emotionally but now financially.

After a few years of having our son, we decided to try for another baby and whilst I could get pregnant very quickly, I kept miscarrying. In fact, I ended up having four miscarriages and I was devastated. I was so grateful for our son but desperately wanted a sibling for him. I felt so alone going through his trauma, as my husband never comforted me and in fact, it almost felt like as I was crying and feeling sad, it was like he was watching paint dry. It was only my own mother that got me through this time especially when I lost one at twelve weeks and had to go to hospital for an operation with which my own mother came not him.

Even at home when my husband was around, I felt so lonely in my invisible cage conforming to what I thought everyone thought I should be like as a wife and mother but feeling like I was failing and dying inside. It truly was being a mother that saved me in my darkest moments.

Then joy happened as I fell pregnant with my daughter. I was so scared that I would miscarry again and had zero support from my husband, and I was poorly with severe morning sickness. But the joy I felt as I passed that twelve-week mark when I was scanned was palpable for me but I still felt nervous.

Then it happened.

Then at six months pregnant, I found out that my husband was having an affair. I felt even more sick than I already was. I could not even go out and get drunk! I had my son to think of and my unborn daughter and the fact that those damn fairytale stories were driving me to stay.

My husband denied it for over twenty-four hours and finally after I pieced together evidence that could not be denied, he admitted it. What I did next was not chuck him out. But I comforted my husband and then I got on the phone and comforted the woman he was having an affair with! I mean, I could not have them thinking badly of me? Even in those dark moments, I was still driven to fix, rescue, make better and to know that I was good enough and I could make this all better.

Therefore, you should never judge anyone who stays in an abusive relationship because me staying meant to me, that it felt safer in my system to stay and get breadcrumbs of love because if I left and had a broken marriage as a single mother and zero breadcrumbs, boy would that be reinforcing how worthless I was! Although I stayed, things massively changed from that day. I was literally in a functional freeze trauma response in my body and would dress in grey, black and baggy clothes because I felt so ashamed of myself, so ugly, so fat. I felt at rock bottom, but I would still put my make up on each day, go outside that front door to take my children to school and when people asked me how I was, I would reply *'I am fine, how are you'*. I hid it all so well from in my invisible cage. I needed people to see the facade of this perfect family.

As the years progressed, more gaslighting, more financial abuse, more isolation came into play. The stories my husband would tell me, became more extreme, like the time when he was eight hours late coming home from work and I got that worried that I called the police, the hospital and even the airline, which ended with him returning home saying that he'd killed someone. Yes, you read that right, killed someone. That an old lady had tripped getting off the plane and he had tried to perform CPR, but it went wrong, and she had died. Now I used to work for the same airline, plus I have a medical background, so I started to ask questions like *'where the other crew and paramedics was', 'how did they take her away'*. But he just got angrier and angrier until I just stopped asking. My gut was screaming something was off, but my husband was looking me in the eye telling me this story. This is what we call gaslighting resulting in me questioning my version of reality and this was just one of many occurrences in our marriage.

In 2010, a year after my mum had passed away and I had literally been living in a fog of freeze and fear, my husband told me he was leaving. He took barely five minutes to tell me and our children and off he went. He went saying that he could not stand seeing me this unhappy anymore like he was so altruistic in leaving for me and that it was because he loved me and hated seeing me so unhappy. My gut again was saying there was someone else, but I was just at rock bottom. I had become the epitome of a failure. I had lost my mother, now I had lost my husband, I was a single mother, and my children were in a broken home and to top it off, we were in over $100,000 worth of debt! A third of it was in my name! I felt scared, alone, and deeply ashamed.

Now normally when relationships breakdown, there is a shake down period but then a reasonable sense of amicability occurs, but this is not the case with a narcissist. In fact, the post separation abuse escalates. The smear campaigns, the flying monkeys, the projection that you are the crazy one because of course, the alternative is that they are a narcissist and domestic abuser so no surprise they must muddy those waters.

I was literally at rock bottom.

I was diagnosed with complex PTSD, depression, anxiety and self-harm and each morning would start on my bathroom floor trying to stop myself having a panic attack. Some days I would win but most I would lose. I felt so alone and ashamed, in a very dark place and it was only my children that were stopping me from leaving this earth. I mean, how could I leave them as who would love and look after them?

I tried reading more, watching videos, and even had talk therapy and counselling but I still felt stuck.

In October 2013, I started a little home-based business using Facebook as it was safe to hide behind the keyboard and it exploded. I was able to pay off my debt and start to give my children the start in life that I wanted to give them. As the business began to succeed, I began to realize the pain of the trauma of narcissistic abuse that I had experienced was now actually turning into my purpose.

I woke up to my life where I suddenly realized, I was living in an invisible cage seeking out others to give me my sense of worth and it was exhausting me because I was putting the key to my happiness in other people's hands, and I had been doing that since I was a child.

What I realized was that I had held the key to my invisible cage all along and whilst no one could see my unseen wounds or hear my inner screams, I needed to stop trying to think my way out and actually feel my way out and process this emotional trauma through my body. This is where I definitely started to become the self-confessed trauma geek that I am.

I wrote a book called *Divorce Became My Superpower* and retrained whilst self-healing but this time at a deep nervous system level. I needed to do the body work to truly heal.

You see, I realized that whilst talking therapy was good as it validated my experiences, it didn't work on the root cause of why I felt the way I did and why I was magnet to narcissist and toxic relationships. I was realizing I held the power.

I retrained with the best of the best and spent over $150,000 on my training. I have retrained in Internal Family Systems therapy, an evidence passed parts therapy, Brainspotting and Somatic Experiencing, both are somatic psychotherapies which have quite literally changed my life and I know many others I now work with. I trained in EMDR, Breath Work, Safe and Sound Protocol along with being an ICF accredited trauma informed coach and becoming one of the UK's first *Accredited Divorce and Break Up Coaches*. I trained as a *Certified High-Performance Coach* with an advanced certificate in Domestic Abuse. Plus, positive psychology has played a huge part in my healing which is an evidence-based strengths science looking at the science of what makes people happy, and I hold a post graduate diploma in *Applied Positive Psychology and Coaching Psychology*.

I literally sought out all the best trainings from the best people and now integrate being trauma informed, with resourcing my clients with an embodied approach and getting to the root cause of the trauma and then with positive psychology helping them live as their best self and experience post traumatic growth themselves. This is at the core of my *Accredited School of Embodied Trauma Informed Living*. I looked at what I believed was needed for someone to really deeply heal their emotional trauma and then thrive and flourish.

All of these have culminated in me creating a seven-figure healing therapy and coaching school with a tons of free stuff from my *Narcissistic Trauma Recovery* Podcast that has had over two and a half million downloads in 100 episodes, an Instagram account with over 90k followers, plus a free and private Facebook group called *Narcissistic Abuse and Trauma Recovery for Women*. I am driven to help people not feel shame or loneliness going through their trauma healing journey.

My low cost somatic and cognitive group online *Narcissistic Trauma Recovery Program* is the number one trauma informed healing program for narcissistic abuse as it includes a combination of therapy and coaching, and it is like having me in your pocket supporting you. It even sparked me to create my very own accredited and certified coaching certification. This was when I created my *Accredited School of Embodied Trauma Informed Living* where I train and teach all about trauma, self-leadership and post traumatic growth with my **CPD** and **ICF** *Accredited Somatic Trauma Informed Coaching Certification* and *Narcissistic Trauma Informed Coaching Certification*.

To date we have had over 250 people enroll on my certifications. It is a joy seeing this ripple effect from women who have also turned their pain into their purpose by helping so many others. Teaching people and helping them heal through body work is my greatest joy. Seeing someone no longer react in a fight, flight, freeze response in situations is such a gift because so much disease and illness is caused by us staying in these responses when we no longer need to, but our body still perceives threat and danger because our version of danger comes from feeling worthless.

It hasn't meant the narcissist has changed because they don't, but the meaning my clients attach to their actions have changed just like it did for me. I even created an amazing *Trauma Informed Self Navigation Mapping Card Deck* to help people see that there are no bad parts of ourselves, only parts with a loving intention albeit destructive impact. My people pleasing, perfectionist, high achieving, emotional eating and self-harming parts all had a loving intention for me in distracting me away from what my inner system thought would be more painful... the wounds of a seven-year-old little girl feeling worthless for who she was.

In June 2021, I bought a $750,000 house in my own name, I have paid to privately educate my children all whilst currently receiving less than $140 a month from my ex-husband. I earn more in one month now than he earns in one year. Whilst it absolutely is not about the money, it is about security for my children and creating a legacy where we can create impact and education around the trauma of narcissistic abuse because it is so misunderstood.

Our childhood can lock us in these invisible cages leading us to be magnets to toxic people. Yet all along we hold the key to unlock that invisible cage. If you feel like you are locked in an invisible cage, with unseen wounds that are just crying out to be heard, then know you are not alone and come and find me on social media, so you know you are not alone and are seen, heard and believed. My mission is to educate the world on trauma, so we understand our nervous system, as we learn about so much at school, but not why we actual feel the way that we do. Imagine a world with no judgement where we stopped saying what is wrong with you with judgement and criticism. That we came from a place of compassion and kindness and wondered what happened to them for them to behave like that. There is always a reason, and whilst this does not excuse abusive behavior, we can then explain it because let me tell you, a narcissists' or any abusers behavior is never a reflection of you, it is merely their projection of their own pain and wounds onto you.

When you change how you receive their projection, you stop being a people pleaser, you tame your shame and you unlock your invisible cage to true happiness and connection. When we heal ourselves, we truly heal the next generation.

ABOUT THE AUTHOR
CAROLINE STRAWSON

Caroline Strawson is a multi-award winning ICF Accredited Trauma Informed Positive Psychology Coach and Somatic Therapist. She uses a unique integration of brain-body based therapy and coaching to truly heal trauma at a deep nervous system level using techniques such as Internal Family Systems, Brainspotting and Somatic Experiencing integrated with EMDR, Breath Work, Safe and Sound Protocol and Positive Psychology.

Caroline specialises in helping women heal from the trauma of narcissistic abuse and moving from post-traumatic stress to post-traumatic growth. Having been through an abusive marriage and hitting rock bottom with debt of over $100,000 and being homeless, she is driven by supporting women to know there is hope.

Caroline founded the Accredited School of Embodied Trauma Informed Living to ensure that others do not suffer as long as she did and her school consists of healing programmes, CPD and ICF accredited coaching certifications and trainings. Caroline is on the Forbes Coaches Counsel as a regular contributor and host of the #1 iTunes *Narcissistic Trauma Recovery* Podcast with over 2.5 million downloads, author of the #1 best seller, *Divorce Became My Super-power* and she has appeared on national television, international newspapers, magazines and radio and supports thousands of women to create a life she knows they deserve both personally and professionally helping them move from trauma to transformation just as she has.

www.carolinestrawson.com

Facebook group:

https://www.facebook.com/groups/thriveafternarcissisticabuse/

facebook.com/carolinestrawson

instagram.com/carolinestrawson

linkedin.com/in/carolinestrawson

youtube.com/CarolineStrawsonHealing

2
NOT THAT WOMAN ANYMORE

ANDREA ELIZABETH

THE ONLY SOUNDS TO BE HEARD ARE THE WAVES. SMOOTH AND effortless, they rush in, and then break with a crash on the rocks not far away. A fishing boat gently bounces up and down in the water, and there is a neat stack of empty lobster traps on the dock next to it, waiting for the early morning run. Only a few of the sheds are open for the spring fishermen, the rest are still boarded up from winter. It will be another few weeks before the cheerful colours and whimsical signs greet the tourists. In front of me, the water quietly dances up the sand and playfully swirls around my toes before retreating back to the ocean for a moment. It is uncharacteristically warm for May, but as the sun starts its descent, I can feel the gentle kisses of the ocean breeze have gotten cooler.

I've rented a cottage on the north shore of the tiny province of Prince Edward Island with my kids for a few days - a relaxing break during our road trip to the Maritimes from our home in Ontario. We sit on the damp sand and look out at the horizon, the sun painting the sky in subtle pinks and oranges as she makes her magical exit. It is equally beautiful and peaceful.

Not only are the surroundings peaceful, but I myself am at peace. I have finally found peace in my life. I finally feel free. I wasted so many years waiting for things to change in my life and relationships. Now I take full and radical responsibility for my happiness - I know that I am the only one in control of my life and I live it on my own terms, unapologetically. I don't wait for things to change and I refuse to settle for average. I am creating a life that best suits the way I want to live it. I am passionate about my work and it allows me the flexibility to be there for my children. It is a continuous journey of healing, learning and exploration - and it is glorious, peaceful and free.

I used to think I had to be responsible for everyone else's happiness. I was so focused on my partner's needs, or my kids' needs - pretty much anybody and everybody else's needs - that I constantly let my own needs slide off the list of priorities. Actually, my needs were rarely even on the list to begin with, if I'm being completely honest. I embraced my perfectionist nature and wanted to be the best in all the roles that came my way: student, employee or employer, girlfriend, wife, sister, mother, daughter, friend. I was the ultimate people pleaser. If I could be perfect in these roles, then maybe I would be enough - I would be worthy.

I bought into the stories that supported it all: Good girlfriends and wives are simultaneously amazing chefs, five-star cleaners, executive assistants, bring home some cash and do acrobatics in bed. Good moms make sure everything is perfect and taken care of. They don't take time for themselves because that's time away from the kids. Good friends are always available to support, problem solve, cheer you up and have a laugh. It's all at our own expense and that's ok, because we do it with a smile. I didn't believe that I was worthy of any of the time, kindness and effort that I so freely gave to others. At my lowest, I had a partner who expected the world of me, but didn't offer much, if anything, in return. Slowly and consistently, I conformed to his needs and rules and found myself in a box. I stopped doing things that once interested me, since that was time away from my role making sure he (and everyone else) had attention and was taken care of.

Spending time with friends might make him upset or jealous, so I stopped accepting invites or he came along. I was often swayed into changing my plans to accommodate him. What I wanted or needed was not important, or even a consideration … and I accepted that as part of my role. The expectations were high, and ever conflicting. If I wasn't working out, then I wasn't attractive. If another man found me attractive, he was insanely jealous and would get very angry at me. It was a constant moving target to please him and I simply couldn't win. I bent over backwards trying, and if I got frustrated it was "proof" that I was the difficult one. He played a good game and wore a mask for others, proud to be the "good guy" and it was often seen like he was the one that had to put up with me, which fit his narrative perfectly. I even believed it all.

Eventually I didn't recognize myself anymore. I had completely lost myself. Slowly but surely, I gave up almost everything socially, as well as my career goals. I fit quite well into the box that was built for me. As long as he was on the pedestal and I was in the trenches, things were ok. I became accustomed to flying under the radar so as not to rock the boat. He needed constant attention, and became downright angry if any of the spotlight fell on me. In fact, at the end of our relationship I had stopped going to most social events. He didn't like it when other people wanted to talk to me and I felt it was easiest to just remove myself from the equation rather than have to hear a rant about it later.

I'm not fond of the word regret, but I really wish that I hadn't retreated and hidden myself just so he could feel better about himself. This is one thing that I really emphasize with my own children now, especially when we talk about relationships. I wish I could go back and inject the knowledge into myself all those years ago - keep your friends, hobbies, career and time for yourself a priority. Two healthy people will have all those things for themselves and then come together and enjoy each other as well. Anyone who can't handle that is not for you. Never dull your shine.

The truth is, I was focused on everyone else and desperately trying to control everything that I could because my life was so completely out of control. It was too painful to look inward. I even tried to control my perception of what was happening. I lived in a bit of a fantasy world as I created a story in my head about what my life was like, which overruled the reality of what was actually happening. I created elaborate reasons in my head as to why my partner was who he was and why my feelings about it all were invalid.

Really this was just one of my many protector parts showing up to shield me from the pain of the truth. I actually justified to myself that my partner and I had such an amazing relationship and I was so lucky to have him. Without him, where would I be? My answer now would be a whole lot different than what it would have been then! Even though it was a made up story in my head, I never felt deserving of it. I'm sure deep down I knew it was a lie. I struggled with crippling anxiety and depression. I now know those were symptoms of the deeper traumas, but at the time, it just brought me more shame. More reasons why I thought I wasn't good enough.

I lacked confidence in myself in general and within my relationships - I bought into society's perception of women and mothers - what they should look like, how they should act and how they should relate to their partners, families and the world around them. I incessantly judged myself and felt judged by others. I always felt I could do better, no matter what it was. I constantly felt that I needed to prove myself and strived for perfection, always. I jokingly accepted this trait, actually, as I always read how it's a prominent one for us Virgos. Nonetheless, now I know that perfectionism really is just another form of self abuse, and it kept me frozen.

Strangely enough, as much as I demanded these unrealistic expectations of myself, not once did it cross my mind that I deserved better in my relationships. My relationships with myself, my partners and others - I somehow had managed to set the bar exceptionally low. I took on beliefs of myself formed from other people's opinions. Opinions which really had nothing to do with me. Yet it was easier to believe the negative about myself and it came to the point where I was happy to point out my flaws before anyone else had a chance. They were a little easier to accept that way.

Whenever something went wrong in my relationship, I was always to blame. Even if I was the one feeling hurt and trying to express my thoughts, inevitably it always circled back to being my fault. Generally I would end up apologizing and comforting him. I tended to push my emotions down to avoid the feelings that often followed - alone and unheard. I was the problem. This was a common theme for years and it reached an all time high when I finally tried to leave.

I had asked for the truth regarding the many affairs that had been uncovered. I was promised answers, yet given silence. At that point, there was so much pain from the escalating abuse, I turned to self harm to distract myself from the confusion and heartbreak. I justified this because I knew exactly why I was doing it - I needed an escape from the emotional pain, and self-inflicted physical pain was the only distraction I had. I was heartbroken, confused and spiraling. I didn't know how to deal with the overwhelming feelings that ate away at me constantly. I didn't know who to turn to and even if I did, how to begin to explain it all. I finally built up the courage to reveal the serial infidelity to my doctor at one point as I didn't know where else to turn. She didn't have much to say besides "these things happen sometimes." I felt like I was wrong to be so upset about it. I was so full of shame and guilt.

Shame and guilt were not new to me in my adult relationships. Neither were the feelings of unworthiness. They came with me as a package deal from childhood. I was the youngest in a large family. I cared deeply about people and longed for approval. I didn't find it, but kept on trying to prove myself anyway, often at my own expense. I was easily manipulated and my kindness and eagerness to help or be involved was taken advantage of. I accepted being treated poorly because I didn't know any different. I didn't know how to express or stand up for myself. Emotions were generally avoided, undermined or denied. I was frequently left feeling voiceless, powerless and alone.

The thing about a lot of childhoods is that they aren't particularly "bad". They are normal for us as it was our experience and we don't have another to compare it to. There can be many wonderful memories. However there is often darkness in the shadows. Feelings of events plant themselves there. While memories can fade, the feelings of those memories, along with the beliefs and coping behaviours, stay in the body. They are carried into new relationships without even realizing it. They are what helps toxic dynamics feel safe and familiar.

When I entered into the relationship with my ex, I considered myself an intelligent, strong, independent and driven woman. I never would have tolerated abuse. For every person that asks "why didn't they leave?", there is someone still in the abuse or a survivor who asks "how did I get here?" or "why did I stay?". Domestic violence isn't always obvious. It often starts out so subtle that you don't pick up on what's happening, and it's so easy to make excuses. I use the 'boiling frog analogy' with my clients - if you try to put a frog into a pot of boiling water, he'll jump out immediately. But if you put a frog into a pot of room temperature water and very gradually raise the heat, he will adjust to the temperature of the water and eventually perish without even trying to escape. Most of us are not thrown into the chaos, we are often swept off our feet, so to speak, and then slowly conditioned. By the time the behaviours are too hard to ignore, we're already trauma bonded to the person, which is an addiction - a hard habit to break.

Domestic violence also doesn't always look or happen the way you think it does. I was never punched or hit, but I've had the wall next to my head punched. I've been grabbed, cornered and yelled at within inches of my face, prevented from leaving and knives thrown in my direction. One time when I tried to leave, I rushed out to the car and shut the door before he could grab me. He jumped on the hood of the car so I wouldn't go. I was absolutely mortified that someone might have seen it happen. I would have complied with anything to make him stop. When he would get angry and rage, his eyes would turn black. He would smash his cell phone, threaten to commit suicide and take off for hours while I panicked about what was coming next. I was certain if he followed through, it would be seen as my fault. There were countless instances of emotional, financial and even sexual abuse; intimidation, threats, isolation, control, gaslighting ... he absolutely would have kept me in a cage if at all possible. Psychologically I was already in one.

When I finally realized how toxic and abusive he was, I still didn't understand narcissism, I just knew something was wrong. He wasn't the man I knew and loved. It was a hard pill to swallow when I realized the man I fell in love with never even existed. It was a mask and a figment of my imagination. When I finally tried to leave the relationship, everything escalated, but my eyes were finally open and began to truly see him for the man he is. I was terrified of this stranger who was sleeping under the same roof. I couldn't understand why he treated me like he hated me, and yet he refused to let me go.

"When did you decide to leave?" or some variation of this question, is one of the most common ones that I get. I have to say that there wasn't ONE sudden wakeup call. It was more a slow build of many realizations that gathered momentum. Earlier in this chapter I mentioned having lost myself, which included shutting down and ignoring my intuition. However, my intuition was eventually knocking too loudly to ignore. It sounds a bit cliche, or maybe even woo-woo, but I would describe it as an awakening of sorts.

Not That Woman Anymore

I began to lift the rug that I had been sweeping things under and call bullshit on the fantasy narrative I had created about our life together. One day, I got hooked into yet another phone argument that just continued in circles of insanity. I thought I was absolutely going to go crazy at the complete lack of accountability, blame, minimizing, denial, the works - I felt so stuck! I walked into the room where my kids were sitting around the table doing some school work, I looked at them and it hit me. What would I tell them if they were in a relationship like this? The answer was clear - "Run the other way and never look back." So why was I still there? For so long I thought if I just did something differently, then I could fix it all and he would love me. However, I was finally starting to listen to my inner voice. Deep down I knew that if I stayed, that would almost certainly break not only me, but my kids. In that moment it became clear what I had to do - break out of the cage and never look back.

I was scared and honestly couldn't imagine what life would look like without him. Up until this point, I had been waiting for him to realize how much he hurt me, waiting for him to take some accountability and make the changes for us to be able to move forward together, but there had been none of that. I wanted to believe his words, that he had changed. They were so much sweeter than the brutal truth of his actions. He told me I wouldn't make it without him, and I believed him. Yet there were still more lies and betrayals being exposed. More gaslighting and blame. He had been that way for the entire time we'd been together - why would I expect it to be any different? *How* could I ever expect it to be any different?

At that moment, I simply made a decision, and it became non-negotiable. I came to realize that no self-respecting woman would have stayed this long. Truthfully though, at that point I still didn't think I was worthy of more, but I knew that my kids were worth it, and that's all that mattered to me right then. Not wanting my children to end up with an abusive partner, or possibly even BE an abusive partner was the driving force and kept me strong. It just goes to show you that sometimes a little woo can be life changing.

As I sit here in the damp sand, watching the final glow of the sun dip into the Atlantic, I'm reflecting on that decision I made years ago, and the life I have been creating. Showing my children a better life and not tolerating abuse under the guise of love was a huge driver for me. I knew that they were worth so much more before I recognized that I, too, am worth more. They were victims of narcissistic abuse also, and despite harsh lessons learned way too early, they are happy and thriving. They keep learning, growing and are motivated to be the best they can be in their lives and relationships, and I'm so proud of them.

The day that my teenage daughter decided to end her relationship with a boyfriend who had been exhibiting toxic behaviour towards her, I cried. Not just because she cried, but she knew what was best for her and what she would and would not accept in a relationship. I knew at that moment that everything that we had been through was not in vain and it had solidified my decision all those years ago. It is imperative as mothers that we always remember our children are watching and we ask ourselves - what do we want them to see and who do we want them to become? What will their "normal" be?

Not too far into my healing journey, I had a conversation with someone regarding a social media thread on abuse. Some people never leave. Of the ones that do leave, it shook me that many stay stuck in the thoughts and patterns of the abuse and are never able to move forward. I had been struggling with Complex PTSD and was determined that wouldn't be me. I needed to become that self respecting woman who doesn't question if she's worth more. She knows. Spoiler alert: we get to decide we are that woman.

It's not as much what has happened to you, but who you decide you are because of it. I know what I want for myself, my family and my life and I promised myself there and then, that I would not be stuck as a victim, but thrive as a survivor. Not only would I recover, but I would be the best version of myself that I could be. I always knew I would help women heal from their narcissistic abuse and traumas, and am creating the business of my dreams that does just that. There is nothing better than seeing a woman transform and step into her power. Imagine that woman is you.

Sometimes we lose ourselves along the way through various circumstances. I think that's fairly common especially for mothers, as we tend to put ourselves aside to fill the roles expected of us, in addition to the traumas we are carrying. It is a lot to hold, and it changes us immensely. Then one day we may come wandering back, looking for who we used to be. We try to remember who that woman was and where did she go? We are desperate to find ourselves again and yet, we're not that woman anymore. For some, she's not that far away and for others, many of us forever changed, she's long gone.

Take the opportunity to answer the question "who are you really?" If you strip away all the titles of mother, wife, daughter, sister, employee, boss, friend ... who are you? YOU get to choose. You get to decide what kind of woman you are, what your values are, what your life and relationships will look like. Happiness, love, abundance, respect, adventure and most certainly peace and the freedom to trust and rely on yourself are all available and waiting for you. The first step is to decide. Imagine the vision of the woman you want to become and the life you will have. Recommit to your decision every day and work towards becoming that woman. If you find yourself sliding back into old habits and seeking out the old coping patterns, remind yourself that you're not that woman anymore and she no longer serves your vision of who you want to be. I often ask my clients when they are unsure of something - "What would the woman that you're working to become do?" It takes hard work and as the saying goes, old habits, thoughts and feelings die hard. Healing is a long journey, but the first step is to choose that journey. Choose you and your future self. Journal on her. Meditate on her. Take on her thoughts and actions. Become her. It can be scary and exhilarating all at once, but know that you are worth it. Claim it and repeat as many times as necessary: I AM WORTH IT.

If you're reading this book because you're in a toxic or abusive relationship, I send you so much love. I have been there, and it is a lonely, painful place to be and so incredibly confusing. Once the fog began to lift for me and as I learned more about narcissism, abuse and trauma over the years, I knew that my journey would include helping women that were once where I was. It was a lot of excruciating pain drawn out over many years. I didn't have a plan to follow or someone next to me who had been through it all, which meant it dragged out a whole lot longer than it needed to.

I never want another woman to go through what I did. I wish that I had known what I know now, which would've sped up healing tenfold. That's why my goal is to help as many women as possible with my experience and the knowledge I have gained, and not have to walk it alone. It is doubly important to me as a mother, as I know the direct effect this can have on children and their healing as well. It's so important that children, teens and young adults gain a deep sense of self and worthiness. Let's give them the tools before they even need them.

When I was hitting rock bottom in my relationship, I've told you above that I still didn't believe I was worthy of better. I knew as a general theory that anyone should be treated better than the way I was being treated. I knew a lot of women would have left long before I considered it, but even with that, I was still missing that worthy piece! I truly wasn't sure that I was worthy of anything better .... but I knew that my kids were, which gave me some momentum to continue moving forward. Perhaps you're struggling with this as well. I'll let you in on a secret: You are worthy simply because you are.

There are zero requirements. You're not worthy based on someone else's opinion of you. You're not worthy when you finally lose the weight, make the money or have designer clothes. You don't suddenly become worthy when you've up-levelled your education, get a diploma or are offered a promotion. You're not worthy because someone else decides you are. You are worthy simply because you are. There is no prerequisite, there's nothing you have to do, say or become.

YOU ARE BORN WORTHY. You can be whoever you want to be and do whatever you want to do and you certainly don't have to tolerate anyone in your life that thinks or tells you any differently, I promise you that. You are worthy and capable of designing your own life, and it would be an honour to walk alongside you as you heal and become the woman you are here to be.

ABOUT THE AUTHOR
ANDREA ELIZABETH

Andrea Elizabeth is a Narcissistic Abuse Specialist™ who helps women recover and thrive after narcissistic trauma and domestic abuse. Using a combination of Brainspotting, Trauma Unlocking®, somatic belief reprogramming, trauma-informed hypnotherapy and positive psychology, Andrea guides women through narcissistic trauma recovery, post traumatic growth and into lives they never knew possible.

Andrea is also an advocate for families experiencing disability. She works with parents of children with special needs to help understand and overcome traumas experienced during parenting, build resiliency to ongoing traumas they may face, and provides much needed ongoing support. Additionally, Andrea runs a charity that offers respite programs to children with special needs and their siblings in her local area.

Andrea enjoys hiking and kayaking, as well as game and movie nights at home with her children.

Andrea is available for individual and group coaching, workshops and will soon be launching a membership program.

You can reach Andrea at:

Email - andrea@mamashealingtraumas.com

Website - www.mamashealingtraumas.com

facebook.com/mamashealingtraumas

instagram.com/mamashealingtraumas

3

UNSEEN MOTHER WOUND

BROOKE BOWNES

I'M VERY PROUD THAT I RAISED MY FOUR CHILDREN AND BROKE the cycle of abuse, self-sabotage and mother wound especially when I see my grandchildren having so much confidence to be themselves, exploring different things knowing I've helped to change future generations and changing my pain into my passion and helping others break that cycle of abuse by helping them release their mother wound and trauma.

I run a successful business helping women to understand and breakthrough their mother wound, old stories, and beliefs so they can feel confident to be them, be seen, heard and have fun and to help them release any trauma from their mother wound that is holding them back so they can feel full, alive, and live the life they truly want. (If you are not aware of what a mother wound is, it is what children often daughters but not exclusively experience when their mother passes on the pain, wounding, and trauma that she has suffered, this can show up as the mother being emotional unavailable, not allowing the child to express their emotions, being over critical)

I LOVE ME! I love everything single cell in my body, I love how my body and mind has got me to where I am today. (Something I didn't ever think I would say) I feel I have found the key to an invisible cage and now love helping others find theirs.

I have an incredible sense of humour, I love that I have now created the life I always dreamed of as a child, I live in a beautiful house in the country, right by some beautiful woods, I love to be in amongst the trees, it's such a peaceful place for me.

I can remember the first time I stood up on stage, sharing my story gave me goosebumps, being seen and heard without fear running through my body, seeing the faces of the people in the audience having 'aha' moments about their own lives was truly incredible, when I got off the stage a lady in her 60s came up to me and said, "Thank you so much, I've been abused by my mother all my life and she's in her 80s and she's still abusive but after hearing your story today and hearing how you broke free, she will no longer abuse me," she hugged me and we both cried. I was finally living my purpose!

There are many other successes that I will talk about as we go through this chapter.

My life today is so much different from my childhood & early adulthood.

Every day I wake up excited about my day, sometimes I have to pinch myself as this is the life I've always dreamed of having, feeling loved, seen, heard and living my purpose knowing that whatever happens in the day that I will be okay, 'life is always lifeing'. When things crop up or cause me to have to rethink or tweak what I am doing, I know that I will be okay.

Life wasn't always as good as it is now, as a child I never felt that I could allow myself to be me as I felt too scared to do so for, I felt there would be repercussions whenever I showed my feelings or spoke about how I felt I thought that I would be put down verbally or physically or ignored. I felt that I wasn't important, I felt unlovable.

I had a life changing incident when I was a teenager and, in that moment, I realised that I had to rely on me. I decided that I would study hard at school, get good qualifications, and find a place of my own as soon as I could. I was hurt and I didn't know how to handle it, I wanted to tell someone I loved dearly but I felt if I did that the fallout would be huge, it didn't seem worth upsetting others over it, so I kept it to myself and buried it deep, it later came out when I had therapy and releasing all those buried feelings felt amazing, something I never thought would feel amazing.

It was one thing me being hurt but I couldn't believe how angry I felt at the thought of others getting hurt, things changed in me from then on, I felt that I was angry like a volcano was about to erupt but I never felt like I could let that volcano erupt and let that anger out, I didn't know how to handle my emotions, all I knew was it felt safer to bury them and stay silent.

I thought it was important to make everyone happy, I often used to say, 'I'll make everyone happy if it kills me' it nearly did.

I learnt from an early age to be a people pleaser, I felt it was safer for me to make sure I did not upset people, as I thought I was always the one at fault, and it became my reality. I became known as the person who always said 'Yes' even if it had a detrimental effect on me.

I believed that if I made everyone happy then I'd be happy, I would do everything I possibly could to help people out, I couldn't deal with letting people down, I thought that if I said no to people then they wouldn't love me, it was too scary for me to risk being rejected by people.

Unfortunately, it led me to being physically and mentally exhausted. All my focus was spent on making sure that everyone around me was happy, I felt that it was my responsibility to help people be as happy as I could, unfortunately it led me to being physically and mentally exhausted. People would often say, 'Go ask Brooke, she'll do it'. I thought that if everyone else was happy then I'd be happy.

You see I didn't think I was important enough to be happy just for me, I thought that would be selfish as I was often felt growing up when I did things for me that I was being selfish, greedy.

One golden nugget I'd love to share with you is 'do what makes you happy,' we can't make others happy, it's not our responsibility, it's up to each individual person to find what makes them happy. When I started focusing on doing what makes me happy amazing things happened. I felt more alive than I had ever done, I had so much more energy, people around me were happier, yes those that were benefitting from me having no boundaries didn't like it some got upset that I had changed, others pulled away from me. My true friends applauded me for doing what made me happy. My life changed so much for the better, I started to feel happy from the inside out and those 'friends' that got upset because I had change or who pulled away from me were replaced by true friends who supported and cheered me on to discover who I really was and what make my heart sing.

As a child I never gave up hope that one day I would wake up feeling happy, excited that I would be able to shine like a diamond, I've always been able to see the diamond in people, I believe everyone is a diamond but for some of us our diamond is buried under layers of old beliefs and stories that we inherited from other people, from their wounds but it's there in all of us, it always has been.

That was me too, my diamond was buried under layers of no self worth, self-doubt, I lacked any self-confidence, I played it small, very small, I'd learnt from an early age that it was safer to stay as small as possible, I was a very shy young child, always trying to stay in the background, I quickly learnt that not being seen or heard was the safest place for me to be, I felt every time I did something to be seen or spoke out I suffered the consequences, the worse thing was, I didn't always suffer straight away, I felt that 'that look' that made me feel I was going to suffer later which just prolonged it as I never knew quite when that would be but I felt it was coming.

I felt I was useless, ugly, I'd never amount to anything, and no one would ever love someone like me (hence were my people pleasing part came in) I believed I was all those things, before the age of seven we haven't developed a critical faculty to make judgements on what is good or true, we tend to believe what we are told.

I doubted every decision I made, I avoided making decisions for fear of being wrong, I was always looking for outside validation as I didn't believe that my choices were good enough or would be right, I would be constantly walking around on eggshells, I was in a constant state of either fight, flight, freeze or fawn. Most of the time I was in fawn, immediately acting to try to please to avoid any conflict.

I would sabotage anything that I really wanted to do because I believed I wasn't good enough, I was scared to fail as failing would poke at the inner child wounds, I had of not being good enough or worthy to have what I wanted.

It was all so surreal realising that the way I lived wasn't the way other's lived, I didn't have many friends as although I loved school most of the children at school thought I was weird, which looking back I must of seemed weird, I was quiet, didn't say much and would be scared to approach any children to play as I was scared of being rejected or laughed at, if any children came up to speak to me I was very guarded as I was scared I say something I shouldn't.

Life wasn't always as great as it is now, trauma was part of my life, I've been around narcissist individuals that had also suffered from narcissist individuals, I was also born with the cord wrapped around my neck, I was being strangled as I was being born which was traumatic for my body, thankful, the cord was released but it caused medical issues for me .

Feeling I wasn't loved, nobody would ever love me especially if I told them about my medical issues as my parents were told that I may never walk and if I did, I would probably not run or ride a bike, as having the cord wrapped round my neck caused the right side of my body to be weaker than my left.

My confidence was chipped away at I often felt that 'not being born properly' was somehow my fault. Everything thing I said or any move I made I felt like I was being judged, it felt like I couldn't do anything right, I learnt to become a people pleaser from an early age, I didn't understand why I wasn't loved I was so desperate to be 'normal' like other children as a child I believe if I could be normal, I would be loved.

All I ever wanted was to feel safe and be told I was loved, whether it was because I was celebrating or because I was upset, I waited years for that to happen, to feel valued, seen, heard, it never did happen. What I dreamt of as my safe place where I could be me, was my worst nightmare where I trod on eggshells and was never seen, heard, or valued

I can remember going to the hospital for a check-up and the doctors being amazed that I had learnt to walk so well, yes, I tripped and fell often especially when I was tired as my right leg seemed to have a mind of its own.

The doctors and nurses were really happy then the bombshell was dropped, the doctors said it was amazing that I was walking but due to the weakness in my right side they doubted I would run let alone ride a bike, I can remember thinking even though I was only about five at the time I will ride a bike as I felt it would make me 'normal' like all the other children.

In that moment as children do, I blurted out, 'I will ride a bike and I'll come back in and show you.'

Eventually I learnt to ride my bike and I begged my dad to take my bike in the hospital for my next check-up. I rode my bike with such pride down the corridor the nurses were clapping and cheering and the doctor again was amazed, he praised me for my determination and said 'you can achieve anything you want to achieve' I looked over at my dad who was so proud of me he picked me up and swung me round, telling me how proud he was of me and how much he loved me.

It was a bittersweet triumph, there was that familiar feeling of tension, the silence I didn't like but was used to by now. I felt scared, confused, I wasn't sure why there was silence or what I had done . All I knew was I could feel the anger so much anger. I didn't know what to do, I felt, worthless, unlovable, unimportant.

It was in that moment I decided that I needed to stay as small as possible to stay safe. All that determination I buried deep as it was not safe in my young mind to show any determination, I became a shy, scared little girl who felt she wasn't allowed to cry. I lived in a constant state of fight/flight or freeze, trending on eggshells, doing whatever I felt I could to keep the peace.

I remember being seven and being outside and looking up at the sky not talking to anyone or anything in particular, I didn't know who would be listening, but I remember saying 'I'm not sure what my purpose is but please let me know that what I'm going through has a purpose.'

That's what kept me going knowing and I'm not sure how I knew but I knew I had a purpose for this life and one day I hope to find out what it was.

Life was a rollercoaster of emotions, most of the time I felt scared unsure of what was going to happen next.

I was swept off my feet by someone who I thought loved me, I now come to realise that I had been 'love bombed' something I never know about when I was younger. After a while I felt worthless, unloved and scared. I felt trapped, 'What had I done?'

I wanted to be free from that feeling of constantly, looking over my shoulder, feeling like I had to tread on eggshells, I worked hard on my mindset, logically I knew I was ok but what I didn't expect was my body to keep reliving the trauma. The trauma stayed with me for many years in my body, thankfully I had help to release that trauma and I now help other midlife women to release their mother wound trauma, Midlife Mother Wound®

It was weird looking back I was always walking on eggshells, but I think that was what was my norm. At one point in my life, I ended up with whiplash and a concussion from where I had been picked up and thrown against the wardrobe. It was like a wakeup call to me, I realised that I was the common factor, that by feeling that I had my confidence chip away, I was attracting more abuse and manipulation.

It was time to start working on me, I ended up living with a work colleague and sharing a bedroom with their seven-year-old daughter as I had no friends by this point, as I had been isolated, I discovered personal development books, I devoured all the books I could on the subject and started to put into practise what I was learning.

I had two gorgeous little boys and when I was pregnant with my third child I had a huge wake up call, I'd just come out of the supermarket when I bumped into a friend who I hadn't seen since I got pregnant and I'll never forget the words she so innocently said to me ' I bet you're hoping for a girl this time?' Those words really affected me, I instantly thought, 'what if I do have a girl and history repeats itself, I couldn't bear that thought so I worked even more on myself to be the best I could be for myself and my children, I did have a gorgeous little girl, in fact I went on to have two gorgeous girls whom I'm proud to say are my best friends, I broke the cycle.

I will be forever grateful for being introduced to personal development books as they started me on a journey of self-discovery, I believe no one is broken no one needs fixing, we are all beautiful diamonds that can shine as brightly as we want, some of us diamonds have at times through our lives been buried under layers of stories and beliefs that weren't us to have but we were given them anyway, many of my clients when they first come to me say they want to be fixed or say why are they broken, I get that it can feel like we are broken when we are laden down with so much of other people's stuff.

I invite you to think about yourself as a diamond that is ready to be unburied so you can shine and be the person you were born to be instead of someone who is broken or thinks there's something wrong with them, we had things happen to us that created those beliefs.

One of the first things I ask my clients when they tell me about what is holding them back or where they feel stuck is 'Is that true now?' The stories that hold us back happened in the past by asking is that true now brings them to the present then I ask, 'What is true today?'

When I started looking at what is true today and focusing on the evidence to back that up then my confidence started to grow. One of the biggest things that helped me was realising that had had a traumatic life and it wasn't just the way life was, many of my clients don't realise that what they went through as a child or in a relationship was trauma, often my clients say I've not had a traumatic experience my parent, teacher, boss, partner that was just the way they were and I learnt to cope with the situation.

We all have protector parts that are there to protect us, there are no good or bad parts, they are just parts. Our bodies are amazing as they are designed to keep us alive, safe, and as free from as much pain as possible, self-sabotaging, people pleasing, getting angry, are all parts, this is how our bodies deal with life when we have had a trauma that hasn't been healed. When we have had trauma in our life it is less painful to self-sabotage or people please or get angry than it is to deal with the wound of not feeling good enough or feeling unworthy.

A part will show up if it believes you need protecting, the part sees you as the age you were when the trauma happened and wants to stop you feeling the pain of the unhealed inner child wound.

Pain is also a part, have you ever had an important meeting or presentation to do, and you don't feel you are good enough to do the presentation or you doubt yourself, you suddenly develop a terrible headache or you wake up with a back ache or pain that stops you from attending the meeting or presentation? That's your protector part coming up to stop you from going through the pain of feeling not worthy or good enough, yes, the headache, backache is painful, but your protector part sees it as less painful than feeling the wound of not feeling good enough, our protector parts always come with good intentions.

I invite you to take a look at something in your life that you have self-sabotaged at some point it may be losing weight, getting fit, a promotion, a presentation, reaching out to that ideal client, what did you do to self-sabotage it? What were you feeling at the time?

In our sessions we delve deep into this and find the root cause and I help my clients release their trauma.

My life has changed so much I used to be scared to be seen and heard and if someone asked me something I was scared to say what I thought in case they didn't like it and therefore wouldn't want to be in my life, now I speak on stage, share my story, I've shared a snippet of my life in this chapter there's so much more I could've shared but that's for another book.

I no longer feel empty inside or wake up dreading the day wishing I was more confident, I know that even if things don't go as I expected that I'll be okay, I have an amazing relationship with my husband, I wake up feeling excited for the day ahead and that purpose I spoke about at the beginning of the chapter I now know what that is, to help as many women as possible to heal the mother wound and traumas they have had throughout their lives. I now have a successful business which I love, there's no greater feeling for me than seeing a client have a breakthrough, the change in them is incredible even their physical body changes and they often say a weight has been lifted off their shoulders, they often look younger and have a glow about them.

I work a lot with midlife businesswomen, working on their, Midlife Mother Wound®

It is great to see after they work with me how their lives change. They have more energy, have more clarity, and know that no matter what they will be okay.

The change it has made in people's lives has been amazing my clients who have come to me with blocks often not knowing what is causing the block but knowing they have had a block that is stopping them live the live they truly want.

Some of the things my clients have had transformation in:

From being petrified to speak on stage to owning the stage.

Having no boundaries to enjoying healthy boundaries.

From having trouble attracting clients to signing up £20k of business after one session with me.

Fearing doing a Facebook live to doing them daily in a way that helped them get more client.

Better relationships with themselves and their loved ones.

Waking up in the mornings knowing no matter what happens they have the tools and techniques to deal with whatever comes their way and they will be okay.

Being able to stand in their own power and enjoy being seen and heard.

Having the confidence to set up a business and write a book.

Released childhood traumas.

To have fun and be themselves without worrying what others are thinking.

This is all available to you too, whatever your mind can conceive you achieve, if you have dreams of doing somethings and you have imagined it, it's possible for you to achieve it.

Many women when they first come to work with me say they would love to achieve amazing things, but they don't think it's possible.

I see the potential and how powerful these women are with my guidance they discover their power, step into it, and achieve what they once felt was impossible.

When these amazing women change their beliefs about themselves and release their trauma that has been holding them back instead of surviving, they start thriving, living the life they have always wanted to the one they once thought wasn't possible.

How may you wonder is this possible?

When someone has had a trauma in their life it can get stuck in the body if it isn't processed which then creates what is called parts that protect the wound that was caused by the trauma. If for instance you are a perfectionist, procrastinator, self-sabotage or are an emotional eater these are all protector parts (there are many more protector parts these are a few examples) and although it can be painful to have these parts the body sees it as less painful than feeling the mother wound of not good enough, not important, unworthy, or not lovable that hasn't been healed.

I work with my clients to help them understand their protector parts, why they are showing up and help the wounds heal so the protector parts don't feel the need to show up and you move forward in your life.

I'm on a mission to raise awareness of trauma, narcissism, and the mother wound and to help as many women as possible release their trauma too and to be their true selves and to step into their power.

I'm passionate about this as I know what it feels like to wake up and feel scared, empty, broken inside but putting on an emotional mask and a smile that says 'I'm fine' to not understand why I can't move forward in my life even though I really wanted to. I don't want anyone to feel like that and now I've healed and wake up every day excited for the day ahead knowing that no matter what happens throughout the day that I will be okay.

Releasing my trauma, breaking through my old stories and beliefs has been the best thing I have done. I'm a happy, fulfilled, confident person who knows that I can accomplish anything that I want to.

I would love to talk to you and see where I can help you, all my contact information is in the bio.

I wish you every happiness that you want for yourself, you deserve to be and have what you want.

I am enough, as are you enough

Love Brooke x

ABOUT THE AUTHOR
BROOKE BOWNES

Brooke Bownes is a transformational speaker, accredited trauma coach and bestselling author who works with midlife women (Milife Mother Wound ®) who struggle with mother wound (The Mother Wound is an inner wound from a mother who is/was emotionally unavailable, overly critical, judgemental) want to heal those wounds, find their power, confidence and release their trauma so they can go for their goals and dreams

Before starting a coaching business, Brooke spent many years in various careers that involved being a coach helping people to heal their inner child wounds and feel more confident about themselves.

Brooke enjoys going on adventures with her husband and her dog in their campervan and spending time with her 8 grandchildren.

Brooke is available for 1:1 coaching, group coaching and has a membership programme.

You can reach Brooke at:

Email

Brooke@brookebownes.com

Facebook group

https://www.facebook.com/groups/theconfidencecommunitybeconfidentseenheardhavefun/

facebook.com/BrookBownes
linkedin.com/in/brooke-bownes-the-breakthrough-queen
instagram.com/brookebownes

4
INTERNAL CONFLICT WOUNDS™

CHRISTA CUSACK O'NEILL

SPIRITUAL HEALING POST-SEPARATION HAS GIVEN ME STRENGTH to finish film school; obtain a trauma-informed coaching certification, and I commit to further development. With over twenty-five years of work in quality and business management, and as an award-winning business owner and writer, I rejoice in all my success. The most significant success I'm most proud is *'losing myself'*. Because I finally found myself. The second - my feelings. Before, they were stuck with people-pleasing attributes. The intense feelings of joy my inner goddess experiences when she fills up her cup first is heaven. *She's in love again and maybe for the first time.*

I'm grateful to have made many positive connections over the past couple of years alongside other like-minded coaches and writers. I continue to build new neural pathways for the betterment of me, myself, and I. My inner goddess, my adult self, and my true self feel. And all empowered by new forms of mental love and newfound psychological wellness. As a codependent type personality, I used to live in fear. After becoming narcis-

Internal Conflict Wounds™

sism informed, I am not *narc bait* anymore. Once you know, you will never unsee it again.

As I look back, there have been many unsettling 'aha' moments. I feel them, process them, and reprogram the memory to disconfirm the negative belief through a trauma-informed lens. I release to heal from those negative emotions that were stuck inside. That pain and suffering were never mine to carry. My body is no longer filled with inflammation related to stress. I dropped twenty-five pounds through cry and laugh therapy, journal therapy, and burning negativity. The heavyweight of bitterness and feelings of '*stuckness*' are not ours to carry.

My ability to break through internal barriers and heal *Internal Conflict Wounds*™ that were idle for over four decades has transformed into inner wisdom and has brought me calmness and rejuvenation. At fifty, I feel better than I did when I was twenty.

I live for *Quality Soul* love now. It means positive communication, respect, boundaries, trust, support, shared core values, and freedom from narcissistic abuse. *Quality Soul* love requires continuous attention and is a lot of work. But it feels magical and free. Because it won't cost you pain and suffering. This is indeed the best kind and enables you to live in the divine, and you get to FEEL peace.

As a coach, I enjoy helping others nurture and build intuitive strength using trauma-informed approaches and quality soul function planning and analysis tools so that their systems feel safe. And so that their glimmering light of the divine can shine too.

Psychological wellness is of extreme importance to me. I have a greater understanding of who I am. Since *e-motion* is energy in motion, I aim to feel energy of love. I continuously look within to learn more about my nervous system and its flexibility. I reprogram old negative beliefs as I travel through new dimensions. And this post-traumatic growth brings me intense feelings of self-love through these challenging times.

I rest with my feelings rather than let my feelings wrestle with me. I used to think loyalty, commitment, and putting others first were important. I detach myself from those faulty beliefs and programs. For better or worse is no longer an option and conforming and binding to obligations should not include concerns of being liked, blame, jealousy, or revenge. This is not love. Love is not abuse. Abuse is abuse and should never be tolerated.

I have set myself free from these negative societal beliefs. I choose to prioritize integrity, passion, purpose, and self-love. Giving to others is only good if you are already full and have healed from *Internal Conflict Wounds*™. This healing is so important to live as your true self. But you must choose to do the work. It is not easy. Before this, I struggled through pressures, burdens, and intense feelings of overwhelm. Because I was always in the trauma response. I couldn't lose weight. No diet or exercise program seemed to work for me.

Since breaking free and through a lifetime of internalized pain and suffering, I admit I was always attracted to the chase of *betterment*. But for others. I was in denial of my 'self' and my *Internal Conflict Wounds*™. I ignored problems and pretended that things weren't as I felt them. I always kept myself busy and distracted. This kept me stuck.

I pretended circumstances weren't as dire as they were. Every day was like *Groundhog Day*. Wishful thinking that always hurt. I

Internal Conflict Wounds™

pushed and sifted through false promises and future faking tactics. Survival brained and *hopium* drugged, with five children, businesses to run, and people to manage, I became self-love deficient.

During the entirety of adulthood, I used unhealthy coping mechanisms to survive. I tried self-care. But let's face it, you can't enjoy a nice hot bath when you feel on edge. The eggshells are everywhere. I admit I drank wine as I lived and worked in *Reactionary State*, firefighting to help save others. I worked for my system 24/7, always dysregulated. The wine always tasted good and regulated my system. I often felt too embarrassed to talk about internal conflict. I wore a mask and was on pretend mode. I felt so scared. And helpless. My system wouldn't allow me to admit that I couldn't handle it all. Internally, I felt threatened with hysterical humiliation from extreme fear of other people's judgements and opinions.

A massive awakening came at the time of marital breakdown. The business sold, my son was going to private school, and I was told I was getting my eviction notice. This huge hit brought all my insides out. It was the beginning of my journey to my beautiful soul. I began to release feelings of worthlessness, anger, entrapment, slavery, and victimization. I lived in an environment where I felt unappreciated, and incredibly used since I gave up nearly twenty years to support a false reality. I soon discovered my life had been a joke. Tricked by a patriarchal program. In this program, after a woman's child-rearing years are done, she is of no value. I felt I was a planned target well intended for destruction. And I tell you, this is happening all over the world.

For many days I would bawl and yell from the front porch. One day, as I sat with my feelings from heartbreak for myself and my children, a kaleidoscope of butterflies swarmed from the field. At least twenty landed on me. These beautiful guides flew over, by, under. I looked up. I looked down. They continued to swarm me. I wiped my tears. The power from the sun glistened and glimmered coming to me. Mesmerized by what this meant, I realized these beautiful guides were gifting me inner strength and self-belief.

Not a cloud in the sky on that day and I hadn't felt safe, supported, and cared for since my grandmother died ten years earlier. This spiritual alignment will last my lifetime. It is the most beautiful experience I have ever had.

After my youngest left for private school, it would be the first time, ever, I would live alone. Alone and empty nesting at forty-seven. My body was in complete shock from the withdrawal. Busyness and stress were my worlds, and it had been going on for over thirty years ever since my oldest adult child was diagnosed with Type One Diabetes at the tender age of ten months old. Now I had time. And trauma.

After raising five children, coming down from a lifetime in survival and firefighting mode was worse than recovering from heroin addiction. It has been proven that healing from trauma bonds and codependency is more complicated. It is also the most exciting thing I have ever done. Reparenting myself and healing has been incredible.

I now feel beautiful, unlike any other time in my life even with struggles through continuous post-separation abuse at all levels. I am a warrior. It is indeed the absolute truth that it is none of

Internal Conflict Wounds™

your business what other people think of you. I yell this to all the flying and crying monkeys who need healing.

I continue to think positively; these thoughts drive me, and I manifest new realities.

The best thing about my life right now is my feelings of confidence and self-expression, and self-forgiveness. Humility is essential as is feeling my feelings. With this emotional healing and realizations that the weight of other people's judgments, expectations, and opinions was never mine to carry, my body dis-inflames. I no longer carry diseases or autoimmune disorders that are caused by codependent behaviors and personalities. Healing from the heavyweight of misalignment and *Internal Conflict Wounds*™ is the best anti-inflammatory diet you will ever need to go on.

My favorite therapy is laughter and cry therapy. It works our face muscles and means we aren't numb. It's the best therapy because it rattles and tones our vagus nerve. This stimulation heals internal trauma. As a comedy writer, I enjoy writing '*Don't Save The Cat*' stories because we need to save ourselves first. And as a screenwriter, I know anecdotes are built to believe that the bad person can be good. But don't be fooled. Believe that when someone shows you who they are you need to believe them. And believe your intuition. Don't save the bad person if they can save themself. This is the only way that the person will learn. To suffer the consequences of their choices.

A typical day includes coffee with peace, overlooking my backyard pool, meditation, Reiki, and writing. My work includes *52 Pick Yourself Up*™ *Card Decks for the Wounded Soul*. Deal. Feel. Heal. I also work on coaching programs to heal *Internal Conflict Wounds*™. All day I dream of healing my lineage to leave behind a better legacy. My healing has brought emotional freedom, and feelings of ALIVENESS and satisfaction.

If I switched dimensions and spoke to my younger self, I would tell her not to listen to negative societal beliefs. Jokes can be real and contain triggers. Flawed characters will tell you about the truth through their gags. When things feel weird, this is your hunch line. Use your intuition and make a boundary. If someone laughs at other people's pain, know that is a red flag. Jealousy and negative attributes imply future pain and suffering. That will cost you your health. Also, when you get negative thoughts, shake them off. They're not yours to hold onto. Don't let negativity relax with you. Don't feed negativity.

Before healing I always tried to build myself up. But I was restrained and always put in a corner. I would get shot down. This created more *Internal Conflict Wounds*™. I never felt good enough. And it is because I wasn't. No woman can successfully raise a family, hustle in business, and look after a large home while she is being manipulated and controlled. Oftentimes, I thought jail would come with more personal freedom. Sometimes I would dream of this reality.

I was in pretend mode with *"I'm fine"*. *"Tomorrow, tomorrow it will get better."* There was always so much shame and guilt from not being able to live any personal dreams. Whenever I did there would be extreme judgmental backlash. I wasn't permitted to have friends over, decorate. Even ridiculed for mentioning camping. I felt shackled. My system kept busy, and I would soon forget I had dreams. I ended up feeling like a heavily weighted barrel of nothingness. But also like a robot. And because that stereotypical *wife in chains* that included food, hotel, coffee, gas, and restaurants, I felt I was

Internal Conflict Wounds™

purposely hidden and kept busied. I didn't feel a real part of anything. Unbeknownst to me, I had a massive identity crisis. Children, business, and busyness, I kept myself distracted from my pain and *Internal Conflict Wounds*™. I found myself sick and disassociated. My body knew I wasn't living as my true self.

After my adult children moved out in 2013, illnesses related to codependency behaviors became progressive. Lethargy and depression, I became further withdrawn and isolated. I did the bare minimum and slept twelve-hour days. Feelings of hopelessness and numbness settled in. My body ached for that pain to freeze.

Conflict avoidant, I continued to people-please. I thought that one day my value would shine, and I would finally be included and feel a part. After all, I was doing all the dirty work and care, and I was the one stuck, isolated, and at home. Wasn't that worth something? Nope. Unfortunately, not in the patriarchal system. Women and children must suffer to keep the profiteering patriarchal society afloat.

In the end, all your sacrifices and people-pleasing energy will cost you your health, time, and sanity. Be prepared. Take care of yourself first. Always.

I do have regrets. Firstly, I deeply regret getting married without being aware of codependent behaviors. Before marriage, I was independent, strong, and beautiful. When you learn to suffer through the pain you will lose yourself. Secondly, I regret not being familiar with knowing about individuals who wittingly and intentionally and consciously and persistently through their own conscience, lie and manipulate to take advantage of others. I did not know, and this would result in my suffering through a long game of marriage whereby I was the sacrifice.

I became isolated from my extended family members. Many hurtful things were said to me. But they were labeled as jokes. My son enjoyed our time at home since he participated in hockey, music lessons, and other activities. But I still felt stuck and isolated and lonely. I lived one kilometer off the road with no other houses nearby. Connections were limited due to power and control tactics used at the time. After all the times I was told it was never my house through various jokes and mean words, my body never truly felt safe, supported, or cared for. Because it wasn't. I feel so thankful for my new beliefs and for my intuitive strength.

Also, with heavily weighted feelings associated with isolation and the lack of respect within the family business, my health deteriorated. I thought a lot about dying. I hid these feelings and felt so shameful. All these issues were directly related to blockages associated with not living as my true self. My duty was to keep my children safe and to protect them. And I did, physically speaking. But psychologically speaking I should have made myself happy first. My tone was of worry, I became a reactionary. This was unhealthy. Also, I should have lived my dreams, but I was stuck with people-pleasing attributes and thoughts about the future. I always thought if I worked hard and put the time in that when it came time for my youngest son to leave for private school, I would be able to live my dreams. Well, I'm here to tell you that hard work does not always pay off when living under false pretenses. I am a witness to that. In the end, I had lost myself. Procrastinating for change. It never came. Emotional presence and self-love are your gifts for right now.

Internal Conflict Wounds™

I lost myself due to all the time alone, preoccupied with *Internal Conflict Wounds*™ and feelings of unworthiness and not *'enoughness'*. All related to stupid jokes that ended up being real. Charmer switches to harmer and jokes lead to insidious pokes. My system felt truth triggers from all these jokes. This confusion led to brain fog, dizziness and even Meniere's disease. All stemming from living under false pretenses. And with lies and manipulations from individuals suffering from bro-code abilities. Negative societal programmed and skilled tricksters and twisters who drink patriarchal poison.

For much of my adult life, I suffered greatly from cognitive dissonance. I was preoccupied with my disgust of intolerable childish behaviors protruding from a grown-up. I was irritated with the perceived lack of empathy and compassion for myself and my children. I was preoccupied with the strangely low levels of discernment. I was preoccupied with the dispassionate awareness related to the well-being of me and my family. Because of this, I soon became preoccupied with my suffering from health issues. I was preoccupied with financial challenges. I was preoccupied with the busyness to isolate myself so I wouldn't be punished. I was preoccupied with goals and hobbies to keep myself away from external conflict. These were all attempts to feel better and hide my *Internal Conflict Wounds*™. Suppression of anger and disgust was making me sick.

Before this, I was a naive dream girl in a misogynistic world. Research has shown that narcissists plan to navigate your naivety. Unfortunately, I followed the plan. I fell for the tricks. I felt a need to people please and to keep plans together. But I lost myself. After midlife and in the patriarchal system, women are of no value. This is in their program. Thank goodness for reprogramming, and I am so grateful for my new positive beliefs to remove people-pleasing skills. Because giving and not receiving will result in a slow death.

Please be forewarned, people with narcissistic tendencies love it when you pay attention to them, please them, and wish to know more about them. Any attention is attention and fuel. Narcissistic individuals also love it when you are upset and attempt to help them or fix their problems. They love it. Tricksters and twisters who laugh at you for being stupid for falling for their jokes, lies, manipulations, and more. Narcissists think everyone is stupid and will cause stress on purpose for the sole purpose of getting supply or attention. Disheartening flashbacks are now lessons for reprogramming.

People-pleasing and saving others end up being non-rewarding and never-ending tasks. Please don't enable them anymore. This is self-abuse. Self-saving is the new way to happiness. Always fill your cup first.

Living in motherhood land can be so lonely sometimes. It is difficult to know what to do, and it is by far the most challenging and underpaying job in the world. Women must reprogram and instill interdependency in all relationships, especially adult toddlers. I lost myself. I felt inadequate, miserable from continuous criticism, belittlement, and judgment. I yearned for my system to believe the jokes were funny.

I ended up in hell by these poisonous triggers. I believed that *my hair was not thick enough. I stuttered from fright. My families were hillbillies, and my friends were good enough and low class. My cooking was terrible. I couldn't follow a recipe. My body was a hack job. My clothes weren't sexy enough, and I wore beige panties. How boring, right? My cleaning abilities were lackluster. I didn't look like Kate Hudson* I believed that many more things were wrong with me and with heavily weighted feelings of shame and guilt, my body never felt safe.

Eggshells everywhere.

I was a wreck. That long game ended when a selfie or my ticket to intense peace and freedom came through. A picture containing a flowered suitcase on the hotel floor was sent to me. This carelessness was the final proof I needed to cut the cord. I celebrated and danced. I jumped, ran up and down the hallway. The shackles came off. I traveled to Florida on holiday and celebrated some more. I had never felt such freedom. The cuffs were off.

After becoming narcissism informed, I chose to go no contact. I promised myself that all communication would be with lawyers. I was not giving up and not giving in. This newfound personal freedom does come at a price and that is my old life. I have said goodbye but thank her for the lessons.

I feel inner peace, internal freedom from external conflict. I think fearlessness now. Whatever happens, happens. I can no longer waste precious time as a worrier. I aim to avoid people-pleasing any character-flawed impracticalities. And I request for help now. This is how I know I love myself. This was the most difficult thing to learn because I spent my entire life thinking I couldn't ask. I was programmed that way.

I know I did my best, and that is my lesson. I am love. I feel light as I practice Reiki and worship my chakras. My body's trunk is a treasure chest filled with chakras. And these are my true jewels. My body does rest on a gold mine. I was always told; You're sitting on a gold mine.

Through Reiki practice, I can heal emotions, remove internal and external barriers related to chakra blockages. This allows me to heal *Internal Conflict Wounds*™.

Narcissists are chakra blockers.

A narcissist will block your *Crown Chakra* due to unclean environments, and *negging* spaces. *Negging* is the practice of giving backhanded compliments and is the opposite of Reiki. Narcissists are *'space neggers'*. Remove them. You will live with the loss of self-belief. Heal from codependency and become your authentic self because you were born that way.

Your true self is curious, present, confident, connected, compassionate, creative, calm, courageous, optimistic, kind, playful, and has intuitive strength built up. Your crown chakra is the highest chakra located on top of your head. It represents your ability to be fully connected spiritually and to all the other chakras. This is your connection to the divine.

Emotionally speaking, a blocked crown chakra will result in a loss of inner and outer beauty; our connection to ourselves and feelings of bliss will not be attainable.

Physically our pineal gland will be blocked, and our brains and nervous system will be in a continuous trauma response.

If a narcissist is blocking your *Third Eye Chakra*, you will not feel seen while in their negging space as narcissists are self-absorbed. You will lose your ability to focus on and see the big picture as there are eggshells everywhere in this type of environment. With painful distractions and fear, you won't be able to get past.

Internal Conflict Wounds™

If your third eye chakra is blocked, then your intuition, sense of purpose, meaning, and direction in life will be people-pleasing the narcissist.

Emotional issues related to this blockage mean not following your intuition, inability to be or feel creative with an imagination, bottled-up wisdom, and failure to think and make healthy decisions for self. You will end up living in a fog with memory problems and cognitive dissonance.

Physically speaking, you may have difficulty with your pituitary glands, sinuses, and your eyes. Yes, stress and living in fear of the narcissist can cause allergies.

Believing in yourself and your abilities and healing with meditation and movement can help heal your third eye chakra. And a change in your environment with the removal of the narcissist helps too.

A narcissist will block your *Throat Chakra* due to the negative experiences you lived through. All the bottled-up emotions may still be trapped inside of you with restraint.

If your throat chakra is blocked, you may fear the repercussions of a narcissist's secrets, lies, and manipulations.

Emotionally you are unable to self-express or communicate freely. Physically, your thyroid and your respiratory system and vocal cords may be affected. You may feel great embarrassment from stories untold. Your inner child may be wounded. You may not feel important or desirable. You live with fear, guilt, fear of betrayal, and shame.

If your throat chakra is blocked, you may feel threatened by your very being. You live in the hope that the narcissist will change or even die. If your throat chakra is blocked, you must heal using your vagus nerve and build intuitive strength. It is like a muscle inside of you that will heal your trauma. Think singing, gargling, humming, and expressing yourself through vibrating your vagus nerve.

If your thyroid gland is unwell, your throat chakra may be blocked. This is a sure sign you are not living as your true self. I had hypothyroidism for many years. It affected my health and wellbeing. I was not living as my true self.

You are worthy of this healing.

Your *Heart Chakra* will be blocked from narcissistic abuse. This means your ability to love and accept yourself, all because of a narcissist's devaluation tactics. Your heart chakra is in the center of your chest, above your heart. Emotionally this blockage includes a lack of love, joy, and inner peace. Your inability to love yourself prevents you from living as your true self and freeing yourself from the narcissist.

Emotional healing will free your heart, and you will enjoy freedom from narcissistic abuse.

If there is a blockage, your heart may be in poor condition. This may also include your lower lung area, circulatory system, and immune system. You are likely inner child wounded and feel unlovable. Even though you know you are loveable, you don't feel it.

You may live with shame, guilt, mistrust, and worry. Your body does not feel safe. You lack self-trust. Unable to open due to the embarrassment. You feel alone. Scared and in need of emotional healing due to bottling everything up. You live with this unhealed emotional pain and suffering from childhood

Internal Conflict Wounds™

wounds all related to fear of the narcissist and your negative beliefs programmed by narcissists.

If your heart chakra is blocked, you may fear rejection, betrayal, or abandonment, including fear of commitment or intimacy.

You may even lack empathy. This is a sure sign of a blockage. All due to the fear of repercussions from the narcissist and their mean-spirited judgments, ridicule, belittlement, unreachable expectations, etc.

You will never be enough for a narcissist. They are never happy. But you can be happy. You must set your intentions because this important work is extremely satisfying.

Life is too short. Learn self-love and unblock your heart chakra through yoga, breathwork, meditation, and inner child healing. This will enable you to connect to your heart and overcome people-pleasing or narcissist-pleasing attributes. Please quit overextending yourself today. You are so loveable and deserve this healing. Love. It is why we are human.

The *Solar Plexus Chakra* is in the upper abdomen and the stomach area. A narcissist will block this chakra, and you will strive and strive to please people but will never feel good enough or worthy of the narcissist. You will feel trapped.

If your solar plexus chakra is blocked, then your power and ability to feel confident and in control of your life are non-existent. You are a slave to a narcissist. Emotionally, you have a lack of self-worth, self-confidence, and self-esteem.

Physically, your central nervous system is affected, your pancreas, liver, digestive tract, and even your skin. Your inner child's worthlessness wounds are related to worry, fear, no value, entrapment, unsafe, guilt, shame, and betrayal.

Healing your inner child and healing codependency will be of great value to your future best self.

Over Eighty percent of health issues are recognized as being caused from narcissistic trauma. This form of profiteering trauma is why narcissists are permitted to bully and they are strategically placed in all systems.

Quality self-love is the best love. This includes freedom from narcissistic abuse. Your health needs to be your number one priority and to live narcissist-free and as your true self. You are worthy. You are enough. You are loveable. You are important. Quit listening to people who tell you otherwise.

Our *Sacral Chakra* gets blocked when we are disconnected and unable to accept others and new experiences. This will include or be in the form of triangulation methods or manipulation tactics delivered by a narcissist.

Things like don't speak to the neighbors, she's not your friend, they will use you and more to deter you from connecting with others. All because outsiders know the narcissist is controlling you. Many married women suffer from this blocked chakra. If you are isolated, you may wish to consider healing from codependency.

You may feel your inner child is wounded and not important, live with fear, guilt, betrayal, shame. You may also feel worried, unsafe, and trapped.

Internal Conflict Wounds™

By healing emotional issues related to your sacral chakra, you will have an improved sense of abundance, well-being and enjoy more pleasure.

If your sacral chakra is blocked, you may have health issues related to your reproductive organs, kidneys, bowels, and immune system. Self-love is essential to living your best life free from the narcissist.

If your *Root Chakra* is blocked, you will not feel like you are standing on your own two feet because of the power and control tactics that you may be suffering from.

You may suffer from inner child wounds from codependent personalities. You may feel unsafe and guilty with self-blame. You may worry and even feel trapped or even like a slave. You may feel the heavyweight of shame. You may also fear failure and abandonment. Deeply rooted, you feel 'not enough.'

Your root chakra's emotional issues are related to survival. Your physical association is in the spine, rectum, legs, arms, and circulatory system. You will be prone to infections and diseases associated with the root chakra blockage or the narcissist who exercises power and control.

Your blocked symptoms are related to sluggishness, colon issues, bladder issues, lower back problems, foot issues, inflammation, cramping, and prostate issues.

Heal to heal the next generation and heal your root chakra so that you can begin to live as your true best self. Safe, supported, cared for, and standing in your own power.

Self-control means believing in yourself. You can open your treasure chest full of beautiful chakras. These are your jewels.

These are the powers that be you. Block anyone who attempts to block you from your health, happiness, dreams, desires, and chakras. I healed and I am a new person, and you can be too. I feel aliveness, and true joy. I am not stuck anymore. Today you are you. Feel you. Be you. That is all that is needed for this beautiful life as your true self.

Flashbacks and memories are new opportunities for me to deal with, feel and heal them with curiosity and through a trauma-informed lens. As I continue to discover my feelings, reprogram that memory to a new positive belief with compassion. I did not know any better at the time nor anyone else. We operate out of our own belief systems, and until we unlearn negative programming, we will continue to stay the same.

Somatically, I continue to heal my fascia. With self-forgiveness and self-love, my value increases. I continue to make amazing discoveries. I feel calmness now, leading me to self-mastery. I am in control.

Be sure to treat all relationships as a business. It sounds harsh, but because you provide value, you need to feel reciprocation. Money, time, and you are all energy. And your body needs to be treated as a high-quality, luxurious vehicle. So, think positively, and with quality thoughts, and may you take care of you. Yourself. And yours.

At *Quality Soul Coaching*, you will break through and set yourself free from *Internal Conflict Wounds*™. From traumatized to trauma-wise you will discover and heal your emotions and improve levels of consciousness. From co-dependent behaviours to interdependent relationships, and with a better quality of life from feelings of satisfaction. You will become part of a safe, supportive, caring, quality soul circle that does not use sexism,

Internal Conflict Wounds™

classism, or racism to conquer and divide. Commit to peace, freedom, and detach from negative attachments. Acquisition of these qualities is necessary in your healing journey to positivity, authenticity, and emotionally connected mindsets that generate quality soul love.

Healing internal trauma and narcissism will lead to a path to your true self, nature, and feelings of heaven on earth. Through healing *Internal Conflict Wounds*™ related to fear and external conflicts, you will find all your treasures within, and you will be free to live your heart's desires. It is all within you. Heal all that inner conflict, and life will be fabulous. Your personality is brought to you by trauma. And now healing.

Find your internal jewels. Heal. Unblock chakras. Finding internal gold heals *Internal Conflict Wounds*™. Remove ill-willed people. Remove fear. Detach from attachments and attractions that require chasing. The quality of design of your new life being with self- belief, psychological wellness, and stability. Find safety, support, and care, unblock that root chakra. Healing in the trauma-informed world happens from the bottom up. So, bottoms up and happy healing. It will be a beautiful *Quality Soul journey*.

ABOUT THE AUTHOR
CHRISTA CUSACK O'NEILL

At Quality Soul Coaching, Christa Cusack O'Neill helps creators nurture and build intuitive strength to heal Internal Conflict Wounds™. She uses story editing skills combined with somatic belief reprogramming to help you re-write and reprogram your story and nervous system back to truth and as your authentic self. She also uses trauma-informed approaches and quality soul function planning and analysis tools in all rewrites and programs.

Before starting her coaching practice and filmmaking, Christa spent over 25 years working in business, purchasing, and quality management. She spent over 15 years as an award-winning business owner and operator of bulk food stores. Her biggest success is losing herself all so that she could be found. Her insides are out now, and she is no longer suffering.

Christa enjoys serenity, Reiki, and personal freedom related to living authentically and spiritually. She, too enjoys story re-writes, somatic belief reprogramming, meditation practice, and comedy writing. She believes rattling laughter therapy is the best medicine. Christa practices positive psychology and can reflect through a trauma-informed lens to rapture her true self post-separation.

Christa currently offers 52 Pick Yourself Up™ Card Decks, journals, and coaching programs. Trauma-informed products for the wounded soul. Deal, feel, heal.

You can reach Christa at:

Email – christa@qualitysoulcoaching.com

Film Freeway - https://filmfreeway.com/ChristaCusack

Website – www.qualitysoulcoaching.com

twitter.com/christacusack6
instagram.com/qualitysoulcoaching
linkedin.com/in/christacusackoneill

5
LOST AND FOUND

GABY ENGELBRECHT

There it is again, the ultimate feeling of happiness, so good that it's almost unbearable. The sun is shining on my face and the birds are singing cheerfully. I'm enjoying a cup of tea on my terrace. One of my favourite places. It's another wonderful Saturday morning.

I'm sitting here with my eyes closed. Gratitude is flowing through my body and gives me a pleasant and warm feeling. Not only about this peaceful morning, about my life in general with all the blessings, goodness and loving people around me.

Living in one of the most beautiful places in the world feels like being on holiday – still, after almost twenty years. Can you imagine having all these choices every single day: lake or mountains, live music or comedy show, theatre or cinema, park or city centre, wellness or dancing and so much more - on any day of the week with all of it just around the corner.

Every element of my life feels special to me, and I appreciate having the freedom to stay true to myself with the certainty that no one can take that away from me again, ever.

I am living and creating my best life eventually. It is a journey I would have never dreamt of in my wildest and most adventurous dreams.

What used to be my dream turned into a right nightmare, I would have never expected this, and I hit rock bottom. But sometimes, on the way to the dream, you get lost and find an even better one. There are my family and friends, my job with the best boss and team on the planet someone could wish for. And then, there is my passion I discovered on my way out of hell, which brought me on this new path with new direction and knowledge leading to an entirely shifted understanding, skills, development, energetic connections, excitement, and the possibility to make this world a better place. My life has been enriched by becoming a Narcissistic Abuse Specialist, Narcissistic Trauma Informed Coach, Coach for Positive Psychology, Nutrition Coach, Brainspotting Practitioner, Hypnotherapist and more to follow, which will now also enrich the lives of domestic violence victims and survivors and everyone who feels stuck in a situation or with thoughts and feelings. I know exactly what they are going through and can give them validation, guidance and support on their way out of this dark and cold place.

And do you know these intense belly laughs that make your body ache? Those have become a regular part of my life I never want to miss again!

My healing journey has led me to myself and the life I want to live. A life with purpose, valuable and healthy relationships;

including my son, who is wonderful for many reasons and will be my all-time favourite person, loving family of origin and choice, true friends I can undoubtedly trust and rely on. I am feeling like I can do everything I desire. I am not only grateful about all of this but also very proud.

So here I am, sitting in my beautiful little garden looking forward to an enjoyable weekend. And, more importantly, I know that I am going to bed tonight with exactly the same happiness I am feeling in my entire body. Bliss.

It has not always been like that. I'm going back years now to a time when I experienced how a fairy tale romance can turn into a real nightmare.

At the beginning, I felt like I was starring the lucky woman in the loveliest and most romantic fairy-tale in history. He came into my life as the man I've been waiting for, the romantic and passionate lover, best friend, partner in crime. He was loving, attentive and polite and made me feel special every second of the day. It was the big love every girl is dreaming of. With butterflies in my stomach, feeling high 24/7. He was a gentleman and treated me like a princess, he made me feel loved and cherished in such a precious way that I knew, nothing can ever happen to me as long as he will be by my side. And he was handsome and sexy.

And then there was the unknown I wasn't able to put my finger on. If someone is trying to conceal their past, events or stories do not add up and there is an imbalance of openness and transparency, take it as a warning! I have missed to pay enough attention to these red flags and things evolving in a questionable way like unhealthy behaviours, which have occurred more frequently and more severe with time. It was a slow and almost unrecognizable process, which appears only clear in hindsight. And one day – this was the new "standard".

Still, I thought he was absolutely lovely. Although he sometimes acted in a strange and unconnected way, I did understand that he had been hurt a lot in his past. All awkward situations in the beginning were around one subject, and that was jealousy. And because of everything that went well, I believed we were perfect together! Occasionally he came over a bit selfish. I considered this as a normal way and adjustment phase after he lived alone and being single for a longer period.

How was I able to be with a man I had no idea about who he really was? Why didn't I just walk away?

Actually, I still don't know who this person was. All I know is that he has two faces, and he showed his difficult side more often than the nice one. If same apologies need to be repeated for same or similar situations without changing behaviour over and over again, there is definitely a bigger issue, which shouldn't be ignored for too long. The right attention can prevent a ride through hell.

It's been a constant up and down, hot and cold, love and rejection, contradicting messages and behaviours, actions and words. My boundaries have been classified as abusive act and jealousy – every time I put my foot down and challenged improper conduct or when I didn't tolerate inappropriate interactions with other women I have witnessed or the constant flirting with someone else when we were out.

During the relationship I felt like I was caught in a wrong movie, and still today the experience does sound surreal somehow. If I hadn't been there myself it would be hard to comprehend. In fact, I am glad I escaped, I am glad I am safe again, I am glad I am healthy. My wish to be left alone and in peace has not been respected, neither during the relationship nor afterwards. There is nothing more to say, discuss or communicate.

In the end, no contact was the only boundary I was able to install without needing his acceptance.

I have learned, such a quick and intense start to a new love relationship is unhealthy and rather a warning sign than a good situation. The same applies to secretive and distrusting behaviour. Looking back on how things evolved, I should have followed my gut and left after he threw his first fit, which was entirely immature, unreasonable, mean and unfair. I was shattered and had the feeling he has turned temporarily into a completely different person. I have been accused of being unfaithful, received nasty messages, which announced the end of our relationship, have faced a shitstorm of insults and shouting. Inside I felt entirely torn. I am an Empath and a loving soul and even felt sorry for the person who had just cut my heart into pieces – without any reason, just because he felt like it. I was convinced that it is important to forgive each other, that no one is perfect, that true love conquers all. In reality, true love is kind, supportive and caring. Love is not perfect, but love is definitely not violent.

If I had only known that there is no way my love can repair someone else's wounds. No love in this world, no promise, no vows and no demonstrated support or commitment and loyalty could ever be enough to fill someone else's void and to convince them that there is nothing to worry about. It is like sitting on an explosive barrel without knowing when the next detonation will start.

Toxicity and abuse can show up in different ways: causing problematic conversations/situations unexpectedly or disturbing events, that are supposed to be pleasant. It can be unreasonable jealousy and name calling. Abusers don't necessarily have to hit, kick or choke their partner. They can degrade and blame, humiliate and scream, cheat, lie, control financially or in any other way; it is still domestic violence and causes trauma.

It feels devastating to be treated like a door mat or being verbally slaughtered by the one who is supposed to love, cherish and protect you. It is a constant change between heaven and hell, the switch happens suddenly without any warning. The nicest evening out or spare time activity can turn into the worst argument, which cannot be avoided, no matter how peaceful it might be met. It can also happen in the middle of the night, a wake-up argument when least expected. One single attack can freeze someone's nervous system for a few days or cause a long-term functional freeze mode. The more often it happens, the more it affects the brain function, body functions and the way other people and events are being perceived.

From feeling like the happiest woman on the planet I went to feeling unloved, unimportant, and eventually worthless, totally irrelevant. I have tried to face his behaviour with love and kindness. I have replied with anger and shouted back. I even caught myself begging him to be loving and reasonable. I felt undignified. When I questioned his attitude, the focus of the conversation changed directly to me, my personality, my actions, and I was requested to deliver a list of characteristics that are wrong with me. I didn't believe there was anything "wrong" with me, and that has caused another verbal outburst and an avalanche of insults. Staying silent didn't seem to be acceptable neither. Nothing worked.

Are you wondering now why I still loved him? I believe in love. I saw the good in him, remembered the happy times and my vows, and I was desperately clinging onto the beautiful memory of these nice moments, events, trips and also closeness in between, which I believed made our life precious. Unfortunately, all of those were attached to some insane drama.

My commitment and genuine love turned into a prison; sometimes I felt paralyzed.

From the outside our life looked perfect and like we were living the dream. So many good things, so much love. Everything you could wish for and much more. Our children and we were healthy, our families and our children liked each other, we had two cosy homes (due to origin and workplace being different), nice friends, we travelled to lovely places, our spare time activities were full of excitement and special moments. From the inside every wonderful moment was overshadowed by a made-up difficulty instead of joy, not understandable actions, verbal violence, and emotional abuse turning into destroying earthquakes. Blow ups out of the blue. I kept it all to myself and almost drowned in pain and disbelief.

Occasionally other people recognised unusual behaviour, and then again, no one is perfect and having a bad day or moment isn't anything particularly worrying.

Every time it happened, I felt more devastation, emotional and physical pain, but I also felt guilt and a lot of shame. I started feeling ill most of the time. Why did this happen to me, why wasn't I capable to stop these events, why wasn't I good enough to be treated in a loving way, why wasn't it good enough what I was doing for him?

Being treated abusively became my very well-kept secret. This included leaving my home to escape relentless shouting, feeling it is required to walk on tip toes, defending myself for things I have never done. Feeling suppressed, blackmailed and helpless was the result of many wrong situations. I felt I had nowhere to go, I desperately tried to have reasonable conversations with no sign of success. I felt embarrassed for failing, my self-doubts grew and my confidence shrank.

Keeping all the cruelty that I experienced regularly to myself had an isolating effect. I didn't want anyone to know about it, one reason was the shame, the other reason was to protect him and how people would see him. The attacks happened more frequently and left me with little to no time to recover in between. I never knew when he would go ballistic next time, it could happen any minute. I was expected to represent the happy wife, even right after his assaults. If I didn't want to hug him or "get over" his fit within a short time, I was in serious trouble. Especially in public, I had to look happy.

Performing the role as the happy wife on the stage of life was appalling. I felt bad about myself that I have accepted being slagged off in such a mean and unloving way for all these years. What would people think about me if they knew what I was dealing with. Would they believe me or even believe I deserved it or consider that it was my own fault? Would I cause disappointment or sorrow for my family and friends? Would people start looking down on me? Would anyone want to hear the horrid and ugly truth at all? After having listened to countless insults aimed at my personality and capabilities to have relationships, I started doubting myself although the accusations were simply invented or based on lies. I call them personal assassinations. At some point they weren't only targeting my social behaviour but have been extended to my physical appearance and more intimate matters.

Everything, that is expressed verbally, can be debated and argued about. Once physical violence comes into a relationship, this cannot be discussed away anymore. Although verbal violence does cause as bad wounds and scars as physical violence, they remain invisible and do not provide any "evidence". Visible bruises are healing faster than the ones carried inside. A physical strike takes the violence to another level and it cannot be denied anymore. Both stay in general invisible for friends and family as it happens behind closed doors while the life that is visible for everyone from the outside is looking absolutely brilliant.

If life and home are being turned into a war zone, it stops being a sanctuary and home sweet home is not a safe place anymore.

In the middle of my healing journey, I am feeling empowered, not scared to talk about my experience anymore. Being treated with so much cruelty, resentment, dishonesty, false accusations, neglect, insults, control – all of this can destroy a person. It has almost destroyed me, with family and friends around that didn't have a clue about what was happening in their absence. They all assumed I had this great and happy life. Playing that sort of game and pretending everything is alright is damaging, causing so much sorrow, heartache, distress, grief, and despair. It leads to isolation and helplessness.

Lost And Found

He was angry 90% of the time. If it was only a lorry driver on the street, a train running late or rainy weather – that was enough to get him in rage. The person who was supposed to be my best friend and protect me, started to destroy me; it was soul crushing. In his opinion this was all part of a relationship, apparently his normal. Very sad.

One morning I looked into the mirror and understood I needed to do something. I looked at this ghostly woman, an empty shell with sad and empty eyes; I didn't recognise myself anymore. And, equally scary: I didn't feel like myself anymore. Where was the cheerful, positive, and beautiful woman I used to be? Can I stay trapped in a life where I do not play a role anymore? My life was dominated by manipulation and overshadowed by verbal denunciation and eventually also physical violence, which affected my wellbeing to a degree that I wasn't capable to carry on like this. It was not only what I experienced. It was as well what I didn't experience: closeness, love, interaction, intimacy, friendship, partnership. Social media and drinking were the interests he focused on, everything at home was left to me, no agreement, decision, or conversation was valid any longer than the moment when it was spoken. No support with chores or other accountabilities. No emotional support. As soon as I showed signs of sadness or overwhelm, I was in trouble. I had to function 100 % without being allowed to have any weak moments. My existence has been transformed into becoming a compliant servant, and I almost forgot how to be myself and how wonderful my life used to be. When a relationship causes more concern and devastation than anything else, it will consume the majority of your energy. I felt either numb and empty or I was in agony. In the middle of friends and a loving family I felt like the loneliest person in the world.

I would like to encourage everyone to have a close look at the situation when a person is leaving a life that seems to be perfect; a charming and successful partner, a beautiful family in a beautiful house, possibly wealth and from the outside everything that appears to be fairy-tale like. Please be assured: No-one is leaving a paradise voluntarily for no good reason!

If it costs you your peace, it is too expensive!

Facing cruelty on a regular basis does change a person. Abuse changes the physiology of the brain and causes addiction (to the good times in between), that's why it is so hard to leave. Experts say that leaving an abusive relationship is twenty times more difficult than getting off heroine – with all emotional and physical symptoms.

I found myself in a life full of lies, broken promises, verbal abuse, half-hearted apologises and cruelty; there was no other way than leaving the vicious circle. I hit rock bottom when I realized that things were getting worse, and it made me seriously sick. I felt systematically erased out of my own life.

The support, sympathy and love I received when I finally dared to share the situation with my inner circle was overwhelming. I am grateful for my friends, family, my boss and colleagues. I surprisingly had no losses. I had their back – that's what it looked like at the time.

I was threatened when I told him I am going to leave. It scared me massively as I didn't know what will come next. Whatever it was – it wouldn't hold me back. Not anymore. I expected everything to feel better and life to become easier after it was over. And then I had to face that this was an illusion. It is more difficult than I can describe with words to get out of a relationship with a person who has diminished, belittled, insulted, tortured and manipulated you over a long time. Some survivors of abusive relationships have stayed in this dark place for years or even decades. Some victims try to commit suicide, some are staying and dying inside. Getting out of that vicious circle can even require to take legal actions, which is excruciating and scary. Although it is more than adequate and overdue when it comes to it, it leaves the victim with the feeling of betrayal against their abuser and the feeling of utter guilt.

Today I do see so much clearer. Reporting an abuser does not ruin their life. They did ruin their life themselves - and the life of others'! Reporting an abuser does not damage their reputation, it only makes it more accurate. Reporting an abuser does not hurt their family; it protects them and others from abuse. Reporting an abuser also isn't gossip. It is integrity.

Sadly, there are many people who understand supporting someone who escaped an abusive situation as taking sides. Domestic violence or abuse is not an argument or a disagreement, it is a criminal offence! Acknowledging this requires to look at the situation and to have healthy morals and a strong character, a real backbone. For some people it is an eye opener and a magnifying glass for situations in their own lives, and then looking away is the easier and more comfortable option.

Stating that there are always two sides to a story is entirely inappropriate in case of domestic violence and called victim shaming.

Violent people do have their wounds and are hurting themselves; they do certainly suffer as well. They do need help and support, most of them don't recognise they are the problem though. Many of them have not the capability to reflect how much their behaviour and actions are disturbing, hurting, damaging their loved ones or in general the people in their close environment. They believe their behaviour is acceptable and they always find an excuse, which is usually based on other people's actions or past experiences. Still, under no circumstances, does this justify abuse or violence and shouldn't be supported by anyone.

Moving on isn't about not loving someone anymore or forgetting them. It is about recognising, despite a heavy heart full of love, that it will lead to destruction and comes with serious implications. It is about being strong enough to walk away as a required health-protecting and life-saving precaution.

Leaving an abusive or violent relationship does not lead to immediate freedom. Nobody knows about the withdrawal symptoms, the emotional and physical pain, the heavy burden of shame and guilt – unless from own experience. Just getting out of bed in the mornings does become a major challenge, let alone mastering to get through a day and go to work. Dealing with any kind of injustice can be triggering big time and hurting, which does cause a completely new set of problems. From the outside domestic violence victims often seem to be fine, the truth is that what's visible is more functioning like on remote control with unbearable pain than leading a happy, easy or peaceful life.

Following my gut instinct and making a commitment to myself was the start of an interesting and exciting growth journey, that is bound to last for as long as I will live.

I am sharing my story, I am telling my truth, and I want to encourage everyone who suffers from domestic violence and emotional abuse to speak up and share instead of suffering beyond belief, in silence. While writing everything down I realize that I have so incredibly much to share, I could write many chapters or possibly even books about the events I have endured with all the sad details, the excuses and explanations for the cruelty, the unbearable pain. Fortunately, there is as much or even more to report about the experiences I gained during my healing journey I am more than grateful for; the new valuable and powerful connections that grew from this, what I learned; about other people, behaviours and bodily functions and, most importantly, what I learned about myself and re-gaining trust in life.

The right people, therapy, methods and education make it, they have been a real saviour and life changer for me. Travelling from a place of despair to a place of happiness and comfort comes with a lot of detours, one-way streets, roundabouts; and there are no signs on the way pointing to the right direction. Being intentional about healing and taking over responsibility is key for success. It requires a lot of energy, stamina and patience.

Today I know I am worthy and that none of this was my mistake. It happened TO me, not because I have done something wrong or because I have deserved it. Along the way I have met so many women going through similar stories, the same feelings that tear them apart and the fear of abandonment, financial worries, ending up alone, being blamed or even accused and losing everyone and everything they love and they have so much passion for.

I have learned that actions are louder than words. And this is my mantra without any exception. The message people send with their behaviours is the clearest and most truthful statement you can get. Listening and believing in words that sound nice and confirm what I would like it to be is leading to avoidable pain. An apology is only valuable when it is demonstrated by matching behaviour. A second chance, no matter what, is definitely the last one.

It is possible to treat everyone with respect, love and without judgement while having healthy boundaries installed, and it is always okay. The fear of disappointing others, the believe, I needed to prioritise others' needs above mine and the lack of confidence and boundaries stopped me many times from making healthy choices for myself. Understanding and loving myself was the key to feeling free and at peace.

Going through life with open eyes and an open heart and trusting myself without the need to provide evidence to anyone has become a safe ground to walk on.

In case I am facing a situation or behaviours, that are not in line with my values or even known and defined as unhealthy, I will look at them with compassion and curiosity, use my expertise to understand, raise them or walk away.

Compromising my health, well-being or freedom for anything or anyone is not an option anymore. My boundaries are not negotiable. This is called selfcare.

I love being connected without feeling addicted, being there for others without neglecting myself, disagreeing with others without arguing, enjoying myself and following my passions without feeling guilty or taking blame. What I love most about all of it? That everything is feeling right.

Awareness and education are such important factors. I am part of Caroline Strawson's network. The Trauma Recovery

Programme Caroline has developed is invaluable and helped me and hundreds of other women to lead an enjoyable life after abuse again. This has become an important part of my life, my passion, my purpose. Prevention is even better than repairing, and this is a part of my future vision; supporting families, organisations and young people growing up with love, respect, strength, connection, boundaries, and resilience. It is a concern of my heart for our society to become aware and responsible by demonstrating healthy interaction and addressing ill behaviour appropriately and seriously. Tolerating abuse at home, in the neighbourhood, at school, at work, at church, etc. needs to stop as it gives everyone the wrong message and has tremendous consequences: It destroys lives.

It might sound crazy when I say that this experience has been a full success. All those tears, the pain and the changes that came with it have led me to the place I am in today. And although I love this place a lot, it is by far not the final destination. I am valuing this precious and exciting journey and am looking forward to everything I am going to face on the way.

Understanding how our system is working, interpersonal interaction and what's going on in the background, experiencing others from a peaceful, compassionate, confident, clear, curious, content, connected, caring and calm place without judgement is as priceless as the freedom that swings along.

The education I treated myself to has changed my life forever and is automatically beneficial for my environment; because of the way I am dealing with situations, the possibility to support and educate others and also the ability to understand actions, reactions, and behaviours. I can exclude toxicity from my life or deal with it in a healthy way if I have to without suffering. The close connections I am maintaining are of a good and healthy nature. Wonderful and inspiring people have come into my life, and I am part of an amazing group of fabulous, strong, and kind women, which form a POWERHOUSE of support, goodness, and love.

The Trauma Recovery Programme I booked and all the follow-on qualification wasn't only just dealing with the abuse I experienced and brought me the healing I needed; it's been like a spring clean through my entire life, set free so much energy and new opportunities.

I have learned to trust myself again, and whenever my gut feeling sends me a sign, I will follow it. This sign can be warm and inviting or tell me something is not quite right. I can entirely rely on it, which is comforting and has become natural. Funny enough I always had it without giving it the right attention. This has become my reliable guide. It has led me to go for good decisions, e. g. protected me from allowing toxic people in my life.

Every day is enriched by knowing for sure that everything will be fine eventually. Every day is enriched by knowing that I can support women who are suffering from abuse and violence and also help preventing those situations by educating young people and everyone who is in touch with them.

It is such a gain to live with the certainty of feeling safe by RECOGNISING and FEELING what's okay and what's not, who I want to surround myself with and which decisions are best for me.

What have I lost? People I wasn't able to stay in touch with. Every connection, no matter how small or far away, that builds a link in any way to someone who abused you needs to be cut off if possible. This is the price I had to pay for living in freedom. His wonderful family I loved very much, especially my stepchild and Mum, will always have a place in my heart.

What have I found? My tribe and the therapy I needed to heal. Health, freedom, love and connection. Feeling worthy, valuable and respected. Strength. Self-leadership. A new passion and purpose. Pure happiness.

Life is full of challenges, ups and downs, highs, and lows. Probably everyone feels lost at some point, and everyone have their own capacity to cope and get through it. There are so many different ways and considerations to deal with challenges. The only thing it shouldn't be: unhealthy in any regard.

Whatever your situation looks like, there is always a solution. ALWAYS. Sometimes the solution seems out of reach or even not visible at all. It may feel unrealistic. Believe me – we will always find a way, no matter what. There are amazing people out there who have been through the same and who will be there to be by your side. And there are fabulous methods available, which will give you valuable information, context, a new understanding, guidance, comfort, and security – like bubble wrap for fragile products – and HEALING.

I've been there myself: in this dark, sad, and lonely place without any idea or perspective but a heavy heart; feeling lost, left alone, scared, hurt, disappointed, let down, devastated and without any hope. Being cut off with physical and emotional pain that paralyzed my entire body and froze my thoughts and emotions. Drowning in feelings of shame and guilt. All of this is gone now.

Please be assured – you can make it. Yes, YOU! No matter what it is, you can get through it – with an outcome you would never dream of when you take the first step! It won't be easy, but everything will fall into place. You are worth it.

Take it as a promise: You are not alone.

Why am I able to give you this promise? If you're feeling alone with any situation that makes you struggle – reach out to family, friends, colleagues, neighbours, doctors, helplines, or anyone else you can trust. If you can't think of anybody – get in touch with me. I promise to listen and believe you, give you encouragement and support! I can help you processing your pain and your trauma and building a healthy and happy life. One step at a time.

Everyone deserves to feel safe and loved.

Life is good.

ABOUT THE AUTHOR
GABY ENGELBRECHT

Gaby Engelbrecht is a certified Narcissistic Abuse Specialist™ and Trauma Informed Coach™ helping clients to overcome trauma and the sense of feeling stuck.

Gaby combines cognitive and somatic therapy methodologies and navigates her clients' personal issues through a trauma informed lens. She provides a safe place for her clients and facilitates their deep, inner healing, to help them achieve the freedom and stability they need to thrive and live their best life.

Gaby is Polyvagal and IFS informed and qualified in the following areas, which she combines to obtain the desired results for her clients:

Narcissistic Abuse Specialist™, Certified Narcissistic Trauma Informed Coach™, Brainspotting Practitioner, Certified Positive Psychology Coach, ABH Certified Hypnotherapist, Certified Nutrition Coach.

This year Gaby also started her qualification to become a certified CAM Practitioner for Psychotherapy and Relationship Counsellor.

Gaby discovered her passion to support others in healing from their struggles after embarking on her own journey to overcome trauma from narcissistic abuse. Having escaped domestic violence herself, Gaby has first-hand knowledge of the impact of narcissistic abuse and CPTSD on mental and physical health, as well as the many knock-on effects this can have on relationships with family and friends, work and life in general. She also brings wider life experience of being a full-time working single mum, patchwork families and recovery after financial ruin.

With over 30 years' experience supporting senior management in a complex international business environment, Gaby is highly respected for her work ethic and professionalism. On a personal level, she is a mum to an amazing young man and loves nothing more than spending time with family and friends. She enjoys cooking, swimming, cycling, reading, skiing, travelling and music.

As a native German speaker and fluent in English, she is able to offer consultations in both languages.

You can reach Gaby at: www.gabyengelbrecht.com

mail@gabyengelbrecht.com | Phone: +49 176 8909 6663

6

I FEEL LIKE I CAN BREATHE AGAIN!

HEATHER BLACK

I FEEL LIKE I CAN BREATHE AGAIN! THE DEMANDS OF WORK, financial pressures and the impact of negative relationships are no longer suffocating me. I now feel I have the balance and positive emotional energy to be a happy working mum without compromise.

"Happiness is not a destination it is a way of life". This motto was staring at me on my kitchen wall for nine years and I kept wondering when I would get there ironically. I am now happy in my way of life because I am living out my life surrounded by people that share my values and positivity. I focus my time on doing things that are important to me that fill my cup full of love and laughter. I have found my inner child again and I can laugh, be silly and enjoy myself because I am not worried, depressed or drowning in things to do.

Day to day, I run two companies that empowers mothers to live out their best life. One is called Supermums that upskills mums in Salesforce technology to help them transition into a well-paid flexible career and the second is Prowess Properties which provides rental properties for women and their children to need a safe space to rebuild their lives. This may sound like I have a lot of work on my plate, but I achieve the right work-life balance with strategies that I'll share with you. I strongly believe that work goals should be achievable within the designated working hours or else something isn't working as it should. Alongside work responsibilities I can now motivate myself to exercise four times a week and see this as either my creative work time or time to decompress depending on what I need. I am able to take time off during the week to attend school matches and pick the kids up from school. I am emotionally much happier and stable as I have focussed my time on building positive relationships in my life. I have built an amazing team of colleagues who complement my skills. All of this means I can focus my time and efforts on the work I love, which I can do within my allocated working hours. I have created a beautiful home and working environment in which I feel safe and empowered and I have returned to church to lean in and thank God for guiding me through the valley of the shadow of death through to pastures new.

I have gone from surviving to thriving which is where every mother should be.

When I was in survival mode I felt like I was gasping for air. I felt exhausted from working so many hours, frustrated at not being able to spend more time with my kids. It was the opposite to what I had set out to achieve. Things had to change as the balance i had wasn't working for me and i wasn't fulfilled. It wasn't the life I had envisioned for myself.

It's important to listen to your internal dialogue and to seek support or make changes if you know things aren't going the

I Feel Like I Can Breathe Again!

right direction. Don't ignore yourself or leave it too late. Think about the advice you would give to a friend and instead give it to yourself.

When I gave birth to my first child I had very few work responsibilities as I was an independent consultant, so I had hoped to take a decent amount of maternity leave but the reality turned out quite different when there was a change in circumstances that I had to still pay 50% towards the family expenditure. The dynamic between myself and then-partner, changed drastically after having our first child as our personalities and priorities changed as we negotiated on new responsibilities.

After 6 weeks off with full maternity pay I found myself working again 3 days a week whilst balancing a new born baby who would only be breastfed for the first year. I was also dealing with my mother's terminal illness who sadly passed away when my daughter was only nine months old.

It wasn't an easy time, however I was thankful that I had transitioned my career into a new job role before having my child that granted me good pay with flexibility as a Salesforce freelance consultant. I could earn £5k a month working 3 days a week working from home, juggling the feeds and virtual meetings and spend the remainder of the week with my daughter. This balance was just about manageable but I wasn't full of energy and living out my best life due to the change of circumstances at home and the grief of my mother passing. I was surviving not thriving and I couldn't motivate myself to exercise so I invested in a personal trainer to help me make time for exercise twice a week to help re-invigorate me and support my mental health which was a great decision.

After a couple of years working in this way my success as a freelance salesforce consultant was doing well but my work started to creep into my flexibility as clients wanted more of my time which would then impede on my days off with the children and holidays. I was concerned that if I didn't accommodate their needs there was a risk they would potentially go elsewhere. I was also finding life quite lonely working at home alone and not having a support network around me.

In 2014, I considered my options of sourcing a more long term regular contract role with another a company or build up my own team and company. Working for someone else felt nerve-wracking as I would be subject to their working demands, which wouldn't sit well at home.

I thought I would solve the problem by building a team of salesforce consultants who could collectively as a group and benefit from the advantages of working together. The vision was great but the reality proved to be harder than I expected and unfortunately it put extra rather than less pressure on me as a working mum.

I had imagined that by growing a team it would be exciting, it would help to share responsibilities of workload so i could continue to work part time and give me a team to bounce ideas of. To some degree it did but it also brought the added pressure of needing to ensure the team performed and we had sufficient income to pay the team each month. I also desired a change of scenery from working from home and the chance to connect with colleagues, so I made the decision to rent an office in London for my newly hired employees. This however generated the expectation that I should be present in London at least 3 times a week to foster a team environment, which was a 4hr

I Feel Like I Can Breathe Again!

round trip at a £90 a day expense. This commitment took quite a big toll and I didn't feel like I had got the balance right at all, it was either team members or my partner that was unhappy with the balance that I was trying to create. I couldn't seem to win.

During these couple of years I suffered two miscarriages and it often feels like the stress was too high and I was trying to do too much. Third time round I was successful, but I felt so sick and tired during the whole pregnancy. I joked that maternity leave should start while you're pregnant as it's not fun working with morning sickness. I was in bed exhausted every night at 6pm cuddled up with my little girl who I hadn't seen all day listening to the waves of the sea outside my window just crying myself to sleep. I didn't know how to escape this reality I had created for myself. I thought if I kept growing the business and team it would get easier as it would be impossible to close a business down with clients and employees in tow when I wasn't in a good position to manage the ramifications.

After I gave birth to my second child in 2016 I had hoped to take a few weeks off and work part time, but when an employee suddenly got offered a better deal and another employee left due to family illness my capacity to work part time became a dream. With a small business and a team in tow I didn't have the resources to recruit an acting CEO so i powered on working full time through sleepless nights with a new born, commutes to London and juggling business responsibilities working 12hrs a day to cover an increased workload and implications created by staff changes.

Alongside these challenges, there was also a negotiation on child care and financial arrangements in the search to try and find the right balance as working parents. We had a full-time nanny looking after the kids and I worked 8 to 6pm, I didn't have any time to exercise and I was often to tired or disorganised to arrange social activities with friends until last minute. I would often just look after the kids independently at the weekend which is time that I will cherish despite not feeling 100%. Everything else felt like a slog and I was just stuck on a treadmill that I didn't know how to stop.

I was drained of energy and since 2016 my body was becoming increasingly inflamed and intolerant to every type of food group I could imagine, so I was dealing with increasing chronic health conditions that became significant by 2020. I couldn't function after 7pm at night and I was just struggling with overwhelm. I was being told I was never a good enough by people around me despite my best endeavours to try and please everyone and to make sure there was enough money and food on the table to feed families every month.

My life has also been driven by financial survival to make enough money to look after the family. Every month it was about making enough money in the business to pay my team members and making enough money to earn a salary to pay our increasing living expenses. With growing the business, I had put more pressure on my shoulders now to not only to feed my family but also to feed the families of my team members.

Running a family business was instilled in me from my childhood. I had come from a very close loving self-employed family that worked hard to earn money. We had always worked as a team and I had had many jobs as a helper during my youth. My parents worked day and night to earn money to give me the best chance of success growing up and I had inherited their working culture. I didn't know any different. This is the same ethos I put into my working relationships and marriage. I won't sit on my laurels and expect things to be given to me, but I'll put 100% in to do what is needed. I would work all hours trying to drive the business forward.

I was working hard, putting in the effort, but I still seeming to fail in the eyes of people around me. I wasn't happy, my body wasn't happy and my relationships weren't flourishing in the way I had expected. I was told to get 'a proper job' and 'that my business would fail' but I was determined to prove people close to me wrong. Since school I had been a fighter. I was told that I shouldn't expect an A but a B or less and I've always been determined to prove them wrong, which I did at 11+, GSCE's, A-levels, university and beyond where I always exceeded beyond expectation. I knew that if I put in the leg work and invested in help from experts I knew I could improve my performance.

I continued to work hard but I had hit the wall by 2019 and I desperately needed to find happiness. On Facebook I came across a leadership coach who focussed on helping senior directors avoid burnout without compromising their career, and her story resonated with me. She shared how she and her clients felt that they couldn't have balance as a senior professional and working mum, but she shared insight about how it was possible to thrive as a senior professional whilst achieving balance if you made some changes to your current routine, changed your conditional thinking, and focussed on what was important to you.

I needed to achieve this outcome. It was no longer about financial survival, but it was about thriving as a women and mother.

I needed someone to take my hand and guide me through a thought-provoking process to make it a reality.

The coaching was £9k which is money I didn't have in my bank at the time but I had hit that pivotal moment when I needed to make a change so I managed to take out a bank loan to pay for it.

As a qualified coach myself i know and appreciate the value of coaching but sometimes you can't coach yourself, you need a third party. I know i needed to make a change as the balance i had wasn't working for me and i wasn't fulfilled. I felt exhausted from working so many hours, frustrated at not being able to spend more time with my kids and it was the opposite to what I had set out to achieve and could achieve in my career.

When we started the coaching she has asked me for to share a key word that would portray how I would feel at the end of the nine month programme. This word was 'happy', but this wasn't going to come without some fundamental shifts that would radically change my life for the better.

I'm now back to living my dream life without having to give up my career. I am still leading a company and I haven't had to pause my career or take time out. I've managed to create a work/life balance that makes me happy, which has boosted my performance in work and enjoyment of life.

Here are 10 areas i've focussed on to shift my balance and boost my happiness which has improved my quality time with the kids and also my productivity and relationships in life and work.

First, get clear on what happiness looks like for you. This was the aim i wrote down at the start of my coaching journey, and I had to make it tangible to really give it meaning. Doing a values reflection exercise and wheel of life coaching exercise was a great starting point to really evaluate how I felt about different areas of my life right now honestly and frankly on a scale of 0 to 10. It was a painful process as it brought up some realities I didn't necessarily want to face especially when I didn't have many 'happy' areas. We can be silly busy to distract ourselves from the realities of life but with this exercise I had to really reflect on what ultimate happiness would look and feel like if it was to achieve a 10 in those areas.

Living out your values is the second route to happiness. Revisiting my values was a really important process that I continue to work on now. I have reviewed whether the people I spend time with at home and work share the same values as me or whether there is a clear clash that makes things untenable. Surprisingly many of us spend little time really evaluating our values and bumble through life without alignment wondering why we can be at odds with people and in our own happiness. It's a pretty quick fix when you open your eyes to value alignment. Once you know what is important to you then you make sure you are living them out through everything you do and setting them as the foundation for your workplace, who you hire, marry and hang out with so you can check if you are aligned. It's also important to acknowledge that your values can change over time, so you may start out aligned with people in your life, but as circumstances change you can go in different directions. Following deeper conversations and over time understanding my values better has shifted my alignment and levels of relationships with some people in my life and work. It doesn't mean you don't have to get on but the reality is if some of your values don't align and are at odds you will struggle to agree on some things and for both people to ultimately achieve happiness.

The third area of focus is to spend more time being creative – I better understand now how I thrive at work and it's not sitting behind a computer desk. I love talking to people, doing creative things, learning from experts to nurture the creative part of our brain to stimulate ideas, innovations, reflections. Previously I felt this sort of activity was distracting me from my work but now I make time for it as it adds value to my work and my mood. This is an essential element for life and work so it's great to do creative activities with the kids as well. You need to find the right environment that stimulates your creativity. Personally, i get my most creative work time either in training workshops, walking, swimming, painting or chatting over food with team members or friends. I no longer need a personal trainer to make me go for a run but I can now motivate myself to go swimming, get on my peloton or go for a walk. I find this time really good for thinking through ideas, talks or decompressing. I've also invested in a lot of training and mentoring opportunities to spark my ideas, connect with new people and shape my business strategy. If creativity is important in your life then make this time commitment. Work doesn't have to be sat at a desk to be working!

The fourth element is making sure I do the bits I love and delegating the rest – One of the things I did early on is get clear on what I really enjoy doing and building a team around me that can do the rest. I wrote down all of the things I do and started to assess what I enjoyed doing, needed to do and what I could delegate. I dissected my role and got clarity on my strengths were and what I really enjoyed doing. Again this can change over time, so it's something to keep a check on. I've focussed my

I Feel Like I Can Breathe Again!

time now on growing Supermums Recruitment and Training and another new venture. Personally, I now love creating useful informative content and training and educating people. This delegation of tasks also applied to home-life and I have a cleaner who supports me around the house so this can free up my time to do other things.

Building on the fourth element is the fifth, and that's about building the right team around you - Having the right team around you should feel energising, supportive and fun. I now run a fully remote team but I have invested in team building activities to help foster relationships and build an understanding of each other. I have focussed on hiring people with complementary skills and values. I started using a series of personality profiling tools during the hiring process and during team days to help us build the right team composition so we could understand our strengths and weaknesses better. It's costly and problematic to hire the wrong people so don't be afraid to let people go if they aren't the right fit for your team. Over the last few years there have been shifts in my team as people have changed their priorities and I have changed mine. My benchmark of success now is that the team and business can run without anytime, but especially if i go on holiday, it should never be dependent on me. For the first time in year's I have been able to go away on holiday and not have to check my emails or sort out a work crisis as I can trust my team to handle things.

Get cleansed with the sixth is about removing toxic people and surrounding yourself with positive people - Examining relationships in your life isn't easy, but having negativity in your life can be so draining and damaging for your mental health. The question I asked myself is 'Do the people around me support me and my ambitions and bring happiness into my life?' Learning about narcissism was a big turning point for me in my life in 2020 and it highlighted some of the realities i was facing in my work and life situation. As a person I am solely focussed on positive intentions and solutions, not blame or criticism. For example, if something isn't working how do we fix it together. If something went wrong, lets investigate and understand how we can do it differently. I can never understand why people would try to put you down, threaten you, bully you, ignore you without any constructive positive conversation or solution until I learnt about narcissism. If you have people around you who try to diminish you, then take time to learn more about narcissism and understand if it's something that effects your life. Be conscious about who you bring and keep in your life and try to surround yourself with people who have positive intentions. Personally, i have made some significant relationship changes at work and life to remove negative people from my life who just try to bring me down mentally and emotionally for which there is no excuse. I have reduced contact and moved away from those people as I can't solve their problems related to their poor mental health, baggage or jealousy. Instead, I have gone on the pursuit of new people and relationships who share the same ethos of positivity and I also actively pay to be work with expert coaches and mentors who instil positivity within me everyday, and this includes my Peloton instructors :-)

The seventh aspect is about building your support network – It was during the most challenging years that I chose to launch Supermums as I wanted to build a network of other mums working in the Salesforce arena and also encourage more mums to launch their career in this space. I was working remotely and couldn't get to physical meet ups so I wanted to

I Feel Like I Can Breathe Again!

connect virtually with like-minded people. I started to build a community which is now 500+ strong and growing as more mums (and dads) join us in launching their career. I love connecting and supporting my supermums, helping others gives you such a lift in moral. I have also engaged the support of other mentors and trainers who can teach me how to work smarter in certain areas so I can perform and achieve more in the time I have available. As parents we need to lean in and ask for help, rather than waste time getting it wrong. Time is of the essence and I have truly loved working learning new things alongside groups of other professionals to provide motivation, accountability and peer support for myself. It is well worth investing in mentoring and training.

The eighth component is about creating an uplifting environment – When i decided to get divorced and retained the marital home in 2021, I bought myself new furniture, repainted, got things fixed and made the space my own. I now spend most of my time at home and have made it my sanctuary by keeping it clean of clutter. I also introduced more photos of my kids, purchased art work and put up positive affirmations that make me smile as I walk around the house. I also have a number of spaces that can I can work from within the home so I can get a change of scenery. Creating environments, you love to live in will help you to thrive.

The ninth essential is about setting boundaries – Somethings were harder to change than others initially and deciding to go to a fully remote working situation was one of them as I had built up an office and team in London that wanted a physical space. Despite the length of the commute I did enjoy meeting my team in London at least one day a week. The Pandemic however shifted this for us; all of sudden we had to work remotely, and we had to close the office down. It has shifted us in a full time remote working team now and this has freed up my time to fit in more exercise, spend more time with the kids and my energy levels are better. With this remote working however, I have created boundaries within my working day. I can't spend a full day on zoom as I find this exhausting and doesn't serve me well. Instead, I block out my time in half day blocks so I have time for meetings and time to do exercise, creative work or activities with the kids. I find blocking out time aids my concentration, focus and energy levels all round and get more done. I turn off email and phone notifications when I am focussed on other things at work or with the kids so I can focus entirely. I review my working pattern every quarter throughout the year and readjust as I need to find a better approach.

The tenth resonates with the ten commandments and leaning into to Christ – Over the last 10 years when I was dealing with negative people and situations in my life I was feeling emotionally very low and alone. During this time I leaned back into Christianity and prayed to God for guidance. I had gone to church weekly as a child and the congregation felt like my extended family, however in my 20's I had gone off to university shied away. When I hit my mid 30's I prayed asking for Gods help to keep me safe, to give me guidance and I trusted the decisions my heart told me to make. I believe I am put on Earth to make a positive difference to others through disseminating empowering messages and services. I have since started going back to a local church which is full of young parents and families which has been a nice foundation of new friends and support after a turbulent time. This bible verse sums up the loving support the Lord can surround us with.

3 He restores my soul; He guides me in the paths of righteousness for the sake of His name. **4**Even though I walk through the valley of the shadow of death, I will fear no evil, for You are with me; Your rod and Your staff, they comfort me. **5**You prepare a table before me in the presence of my enemies. You anoint my head with oil; my cup overflows **Psalm 23.4**

With all of these strategies in place I am now even more financially successful than I was before. I am no longer fighting for financial survival, but I am thriving financially and able to provide for my family and my team's family. I now realise that I was focussing my time and energy in the wrong places, and there were certain areas of my life where my energy was getting drained. Making the shifts has made me happier all round and people remark that I am glowing. I love that I have time to do what I love at work, spend time with my kids, exercise more often and my chronic health condition which was diagnosed as Endometriosis has massively improved since having an operation, reducing my stress, improving my well-being and managing my diet. I feel like I can breathe again and the tightness I felt in my chest has disappeared. This freedom manifests physically as I can now swim a whole of length at the pool without coming up for air which I couldn't do before.

An aspect I am thankful for throughout this whole period of life is my ability to be financially independent which has helped me to make changes and choices that might have been much harder for me to make if I didn't have my own income. Having a Salesforce career has given me the financial security and it is the reason why I am so passionate about sharing it with other mothers, especially those that need to build their own financial stability.

However having a job doesn't automatically create happiness. Learning how to achieve flexibility and balance in a career takes considered effort, as we have to implement our own boundaries and manifest our own values in how we work to achieve happiness.

I now teach mothers on our Supermums Courses not only Salesforce skills but also the coaching skills to help them manage their professional career as it's important they thrive not survive. I love my job helping other mums improve their own financial situation and work-life balance. Many of our trainees tell me how much our programme has changed their life, and it is so rewarding.

If you are looking to looking to thrive in your career and life as a career mum then please do reach out to us at www.supermums.org

ABOUT THE AUTHOR
HEATHER BLACK

Heather Black is a professional coach and social entrepreneur. She focusses on empowering women to achieve emotional and financial stability through her two businesses.

Supermums, is a global brand, established to support women to upskill and secure a flexible well-paid role within the Salesforce sector.

Prowess Properties invests in property to provide rental homes to women looking to rebuild their homes after hardship.

As a woman she has navigated and overcome multiple challenges in her life including divorce, a change in career, entrepreneurship business challenges, loss of both parents, closure of a business during the pandemic, and chronic health issues caused by endometriosis and stress.

Life isn't a walk in the park but if she believes that if surround yourself with the right support it is possible to bounce back from anything. Together we are stronger then working alone.

If you are looking to looking to thrive in your career and life as a career mum then please do reach out to us at www.super-mums.org

7

ASSAULT OF THE HEART

HOUA UTECH

"There is no greater agony than bearing an untold story inside you."

— *MAYA ANGELOU*

THROUGH THE SECRETS AND THE LIES, THE TEARS AND THE heartbreak, and the painful grief process, I was determined to find my way back to myself. My determination led me down an unexpected path but a necessary one. At the start of my healing, it took every bit of me to gather up the energy and courage to face each day. My body and mind were overtaken by the heaviness of the trauma. As I cycled in and out of anxiety, shame, guilt, overwhelm, and fatigue, fear settled in as the norm. My whole system was worn down and depleted of energy from being in survival mode. I did not feel safe in the world, and I knew I had to start here. I needed to create safety and security in my world. I was born into a life of survival, but this was beyond anything I had ever experienced before.

It was a process to get here and it's important to remember that *here* is an ever-evolving point. Covert narcissistic abuse is intentional. Covert narcissistic abusers are strategic and patterned in their behaviors. I lost so much of myself and one of the hardest realizations was uncovering their intentional and strategic attempts to destroy my heart, destroy my mind, and destroy the relationship I had with people and the world around me.

As I sit here today, it is an incredible feeling to be present in my body again – to be able to talk and laugh freely; to move with energy and dance around with ease; to enjoy time with family and friends; to feel the excitement that comes with meeting new people; to be in the present moment; to live with wonder and possibilities, and to love from a place of peace and gratitude.

I found my way back to myself.

Growing up, I didn't have any models of healthy relationships. I grew up in a home as a first-generation-born Hmong girl. My family fled their homeland of Laos at the close of the Vietnam War. They found safety in the refugee camps in Thailand before being relocated to New York State by the United States Government. My family arrived in the United States in 1979 and I was born shortly after.

At three years old, my mother passed away unexpectedly from complications of a staph infection. In her short time of living in the U.S., my mother had delivered four children, in addition to my older brother who was born in the refugee camps in Thailand. She had adrenal cancer during her last pregnancy and gave birth to my brother prematurely via cesarean section. Due to her weakened system and complications, she passed away two months later from a staph infection.

I have no memories of my mother. I only have borrowed memories from my grandfather, my aunts, and my uncles. Regardless, I have always felt her presence around me. I have kept her close to me, supporting me, protecting me, and guiding me. Whether it was in the day-to-day, struggling during a painful time, or celebrating a joy or accomplishment in my life, she has been with me.

Losing my mother at three years old and then later getting cut off from my maternal grandparents left an emptiness in my life. It created instability and insecurity for me as I was left to fill in the blanks, as a five year old. My grandparent's home provided warmth, safety, and love, and was the only place where I got to see my mother's face. They were the only ones who had pictures of her and shared stories of her. They cried every time I saw them. They openly grieved her and grieved for me and my siblings as well. They were my only source of connection to my mother and I hung onto those visits.

I had lived a sheltered life. I was raised in a culture where boys were valued, and girls were married off. As a child, I learned the importance of listening, and I learned to be aware of my surroundings, observing everyone and everything around me. I was the second oldest, so I very quickly moved into a parentified role, with the expectation that I would cook, clean, and take care of my siblings.

In my early teen years, afterschool clubs and activities piqued my interest, but I was banned from participating. I envied my friends who were given the freedom to participate. There was a carefree vibe that I saw in most kids my age. They would joke around and laugh while I rarely said a word at school. I was a wallflower and a follower and I was okay with that. The last thing I wanted was to be noticed. I didn't want to get noticed by the teachers or from other students at school. I observed everything around me but lived quietly in my head.

As I entered my high school years, there were big shifts in the dynamics of my home life. I no longer felt safe at home due to the increase in volatility. The mood of the whole house would shift depending on who was home. I quickly learned in order to get around the abuse, I had to be as quiet as possible. I had to silence my voice and silence my movements. Most days, I would be still for hours in my room as my system was on high alert. I learned to track movements throughout the whole house. I could gauge when the house was full of anger and when there was peace. I learned to adjust my days and nights based on the mood of the movements throughout the house. I developed a heightened sense of awareness and learned to survive by appearing invisible.

Freedom and peace came in the form of daydreaming. I would sit for hours on end, daydreaming and wishing for the freedom to experience life outside of my four bedroom walls.

I dreamt of a life filled with adventure. I wanted to explore the world and meet people of different cultures. I dreamt of meeting a man who would save me from this life. And ultimately, my biggest desire was to become a mother. I wanted to have a houseful of children. I loved the idea of raising a family and fully immersing myself in the day-to-day moments with them. I wanted nothing more than to raise children in a safe and loving home and to be able to experience life with them. My daydreams were colourful, detailed, and full of adventure. I would get lost for hours in my hopes and dreams for the future as I sat in the quiet and safety of my room.

My childhood experiences were traumatic and undoubtedly left me feeling unsafe and vulnerable in life and relationships. My core wounds of not feeling seen, not feeling good enough, and not feeling loveable were reminiscent in my significant love relationships. As my system worked to avoid feeling unseen, not enough, and unloveable, the protective parts of me took over.

In my relationships, I became a caretaker, a people-pleaser, accommodating, happy, positive, safety-conscious, a planner, driven to achieve, a therapizer, and more. I was focused on making sure I made the right decisions every step of the way. These protector parts showed up in how I viewed myself and the ways I engaged with others. They also showed up in the types of relationships I was drawn to. It was easy for me to get lost in relationships as I navigated between what was best for the relationship and what made sense to me. Ultimately, these lessons helped me with my practice of grounding my body, connecting with my intuition, and allowing that to lead me back to safety and back to my inner self. As an empath, I have learned to trust my strong intuitive sense and can pick up on the feelings and emotions of people and situations around me.

I started my career as a social worker in organizations, focused on providing services, education, and advocacy for children, youth, women, and families. My life and career have shifted over the last nineteen years, but I remain committed to working with women and families. I know first-hand the psychological, sexual, physical, financial, and spiritual abuse from individuals, groups of people, and systems. The trauma that comes from abuse often creates a devastating hold on a person's overall health and quality of life.

In my search to understand and heal, I realized that many therapists, social workers, court professionals, and human service organizations are not well-informed about coercive control. Coercive control is the foundation of domestic abuse and includes psychological abuse, emotional abuse, financial abuse, and abuse by proxy, which is the harmful and manipulative use of children to further control and hurt the victim. Coercive control has become recognized in several states in the United States but it is imperative for all states to adopt laws criminalizing coercive control. Coercive control not only impacts women but also negatively impacts the children who bear witness to the power, control, and abuse.

It is my mission to bring awareness, education, and healing resources to individuals, families, organizations, and communities because abuse and trauma are largely misunderstood, misdiagnosed, and hence, go untreated. As a Trauma-Informed Specialist, I provide 1:1 client work and will soon be offering group work. I am also the host of the podcast, *This Emboldened Life*, which focuses on providing education, resources, survivor stories, expert interviews, and community for women impacted by coercive control, covert narcissistic abuse, betrayal trauma, divorce/post-separation abuse, and abuse by systems and professionals associated with the family court system. Episodes for *This Emboldened Life* will be released in October 2022.

There is energy, strength, and power when women come together with a mission to create change in the world. I am a member of the *National Safe Parents Organization*, a coalition of more than 100,000 survivor parents and concerned citizens in the United States advocating for evidence-based policies which put child safety at the forefront of child custody decisions. I am a founding member and provide support to *Wisconsin Safe Parents*, a group committed to bringing awareness and change, at the state level, to protect children in child custody cases.

Death by a thousand cuts.

I love 'love'. I love being in love. I easily forgive and I easily can move beyond issues that surface in my relationships. That doesn't mean I am someone who sweeps issues under the rug, in fact, it is quite the contrary.

With each betrayal, I actively worked to understand the situation so I could make sense of it for myself, in hopes I could save the relationship. My execution wasn't always perfect, but I strongly believe by confronting the issues head-on that I would be able to help the other person get to the core of their personal struggles and heal.

Relationships are complex and when hope, love, the search for a soul mate, and fairy tale endings become the norm in society, it makes navigating relationship dynamics even more complicated.

How many betrayals does it take before you decide to walk away?

One, right? Or maybe it depends on the type of betrayals?

What if the first betrayal was just an *innocent* texting relationship between your partner and his female colleague who he often described as a 'sister'? Does it matter if the texts occurred during the day or if they occurred at all hours of the night? What if you saw messages showcasing their lack of boundaries or their extensive need to give emotional support and validation? Are they strictly friends? Or would this be enough to end your relationship?

Let's say your partner later reveals he was intimate with another woman but said he had no intentions of ever seeing her again. He is openly emotional and begs for your forgiveness. He says he was feeling lonely and vulnerable because he was having issues with work. He emphasizes it was the biggest mistake of his life…that is, aside from his other indiscretions. But he insists he will never do it again.

What would you do?

Your head is saying, "He is a serial cheater and will never change. This is proof." Your heart is empathizing, "He was crying so he must feel bad for what he did. I know how stressful his job is." Then your gut is signalling, "Something doesn't feel right in my body."

Life decisions are rarely clear-cut. Then you factor in the parts that may show up in these situations such as anger, indecision, anxiety, caretaking, self-doubt, and inner critic, making decisions may feel impossible. These protector parts show up because they are sensing there's a threat to your system. They are doing their best to protect you from feeling the deep pain of your childhood wounds, such as not feeling worthy, not feeling good enough, and/or not feeling loveable. Everyone has parts. Parts are normal and make up the different aspects of our personalities. As you work to heal your parts, be gentle and kind with yourself as you work to regulate your nervous system. Shifting your system away from a freeze, fight, or flight state will help to calm your body and its responses. As you work with this practice, have patience and trust the new awarenesses you gain from the connection between your mind, body, and intuition.

Betrayal trauma is insidious. It comes with layers of secrecy, lies, deceit, psychological manipulation, neglect, blame, rejection, abuse based in entitlements, and harm to a person's overall health. This can break down a person's boundaries, takes away their safeguards, and strips them of their intuitive senses. This creates a pattern of her questioning her own sense of reality as she dismisses her thoughts and feelings, to eventually adapt and rely on her abuser's crafted reality.

As a single woman in my twenties, I was independent, and I was confident in the work I was doing. I would sometimes lean towards being more reserved in new situations but in general, I was outgoing. I enjoyed meeting new people and learning about them. I enjoyed building relationships, socializing with friends, and being with family. I liked socializing and I also valued having my alone time. The alone time helped me slow down so I could be present with my thoughts and get grounded. I appreciated having full autonomy as a single woman.

I met a lot of guys, but I was quick to place them in the friend zone. The idea of starting a relationship as a *slow burn* didn't excite me. Instead, I was drawn to relationships that started as *intense flames*, all-consuming, exhilarating, and intoxicating. When I fell for someone, I would fall hard. And when I committed myself to these relationships, I was often left brokenhearted. I was attracted to guys who were charming, smart, witty, and adventurous. On a deeper level, I looked for guys who shared similar views on issues such as politics, religion, culture, and values.

There were always red flags. Even when they looked great on paper, I was left to question their character and their intentions as my intuitive senses would buzz with worry. Within weeks of getting to know some, I would feel uncomfortable with their questionable relationship history – revealing a consistent history of cheating or engagement in high-risk behaviors that were over and above the average person's. To counteract my worry, I would tell myself it was too early to make a decision on their character and that I'd need more time to get to know them. Part of me would question if I was being too judgemental. Another part of me would question if I was self-sabotaging myself out of fear of being unloveable. I would eventually buy into whatever story they convinced me of, as they worked to portray themselves in the best way possible.

This is when I, unknowingly, would start to quiet my intuition in my relationships.

I wish I had learned what it meant to listen and trust my intuition. Identifying red flags has become a common way to alert us when deciding whether someone's actions and behaviours are concerning.

For example, a common Red Flag checklist may ask:

- Does he make you a priority?
- Does he return your phone calls or messages in a timely manner?
- Does he try to control your friendships and family relationships?
- Does he apologize after an argument?

There are major problems with the questions. First, it's likely we will try to find the exception to the rule for each of these questions. Second, the questions tend to be more indicative of overt abuse—which emphasizes physical aggression and overlooks the covert acts of abuse. It is important to note that when we use an arbitrary checklist to decipher whether the number of red flags is enough to halt the relationship, we end up ignoring a significant part of our system – our gut instincts. A key component in our healing journey is working to open up our awareness of how our body responds in those moments. In doing so, we begin to nurture and develop a relationship with our intuition. Our intuition is shaped by our sensory experiences and that's useful in helping to guide us as we gauge if something is safe for our system.

I believed the stories, the lies, and the crumbs of love because that gave me hope. I was willing to sacrifice my own health and happiness to save another's soul. I was so full of confusion, full of fear, and so desperately grasped for any remnants of what was when my relationships ended.

I was persistent in my relationships but the flame eventually burns out. And when that happened, all that would beeft would be a shell of a shattered self.

I no longer had the energy to focus on others. I had no desire to ask questions about relationships. I no longer cared to share about myself. I neglected my physical, mental, and emotional needs. I stopped trusting my intuition. I stopped trusting my ideas, thoughts, feelings, and my heart. I quieted the passion and purpose in my voice. I stopped dreaming for myself. I stopped engaging with most people. I tamed my passion. I became detached from my physical being. I was floating outside of myself. I stopped having awareness of the world around me.

There were days when all I did was cry. There were days when I felt completely numb and detached. And that was okay.

Grief is good. I am grateful for the friends and family who would check in on me regularly, making sure I was okay. They made sure I was eating, sleeping, and making attempts to leave the house. When my body is under stress, I tend to lose weight. It's guaranteed that my eyes will have permanent bags. I generally look and feel miserable. It's not pretty, it's not fun but it's all been necessary for me as I worked to heal.

In my healing process, the best thing I did was to allow myself to fully feel the pain and grief inside of me. Whether I was alone or with a trusted friend or family member, I cried, sometimes screamed, and fully expressed my frustrations about the injustices I felt. I didn't try to control it or hold back, I let the emotions out as they needed to come out. Betrayal, in its many forms, fit perfectly into the wounds of my childhood of not feeling seen, not feeling enough, and not feeling loveable. It would've been easy to allow the pain and the unworthiness feelings to settle in as my new reality, but my inner voice refused to let that be. Hope, along with love, purpose, passion, compassion, courage, and determination stayed at the forefront, giving me the strength to release the pain and heal the brokenness of my heart.

Meaning matters. I can look back and appreciate the meaningful moments I had in my relationships. I carry those memories with me because they were real to me. No one gets to take those memories away from me. In those moments, I showed up in my most authentic way, true to form, and with the best of intentions. In those memories, it no longer matters who the other person was. The way I shared my love and my vulnerabilities are what matters.

I love with my whole heart. And when it's met with heartbreak, it can feel like it's been shattered into a million little pieces.

The grief from any abrupt end of a relationship is challenging so allow yourself kindness and grace as you begin to heal. Take things slow and at your own pace. Allow your body to rest and recover. With time, you will take the steps necessary to move forward.

When you are ready, here is a process to guide your healing:

Set an *intention*. An intention will keep you focused and keep you going. Keep it simple. I was focused on pulling through the pain and coming out stronger and healthier. I didn't fully believe it at first, but I willed myself to keep saying it until it became the only thing I believed.

Create *connection and safety*. Relationships are the greatest assets in our journey. Betrayal can make it difficult to move forward, especially when it caused by more than one person, a family of people, or a community. So, identify a few of your trusted friends and family members. It's important to evaluate and keep close to you the people who are invested in your healing and growth.

Open up your *awareness through education*. Keep in mind that it can be easy to get consumed by information on social media. There is value in learning about abuse so you can gain awareness about how you got to this point. It was eye-opening for me and spoke directly to what I had experienced in my life. Knowledge is power and takes in the ways in which the information will best prepare you going forward.

Access *resources*. Building a *kundalini meditation* practice was the first thing I did to help balance out the blocked chakras in my body. This is a powerful practice for anyone recovering from betrayal trauma. Kundalini is a practice used to awaken your spiritual energy located at the base of your spine. The energy then travels through the seven chakras or energy centers, throughout your body, cleansing and revitalizing you.

Along with kundalini meditations and breathwork, learning about feminine and masculine energy will help to support the balance of both energies within your body. We are made up of both of these energies. Feminine energy is comprised of Divine, Wounded, and Toxic energy. When you are functioning from your *Divine* feminine energy, you feel at flow, creating, manifesting, birthing, playful, intuitive, and surrendering. Whereas, *Wounded* feminine energy presents as co-dependency, over-emotional, and powerlessness. When you carry *Toxic* feminine energy, it shows as insecurity, victimhood, desperation, judging, and criticism.

Masculine energy is comprised of Divine, Wounded, and Toxic energy too. When you are functioning from your *Divine* masculine, your energy consists of stillness, presence, responsiveness, groundedness, steadiness, protectiveness, safety, supportive and integrity. Whereas, *Wounded* masculine energy presents as abuse of power, dominance, high need to control, abuse, and perpetrator energy. *Toxic* masculine energy is competitive, cold, distant, withdrawn, blaming, shaming, aggressive, and prideful. It is important to identify and also harness both Divine feminine and Divine masculation energy.

Brainspotting is another resource that helped move me beyond the fight/freeze/fawn states. It offered me relief from talk therapy and instead helped me build a stronger relationship with the sensations in my body, in order to help release the trauma.

Embodiment Practices- With doing regular Brainspotting and Kundalini breathwork, I started feeling major energetic shifts in my body. My body and mood started to feel lighter and brighter. I felt more attuned to the sensations in my body which helped to strengthen my intuition.

Self-leadership - As I gained clarity in my healing process, I wanted to keep building on my knowledge and skills by becoming a *Certified Narcissistic Abuse Specialist & an Accredited Integrated Trauma Informed Coach*. I was determined to keep working with women to help them reclaim their lives.

Straight away, I was determined to be freed from the abuse and heal from the trauma I had endured. The greatest feeling is in knowing I did not have to heal my heart, my mind, my body, and my spirit all on my own. It's been incredibly beautiful and uplifting to know there is a whole community of women ready to stand alongside any one of us when needed. Together, we are building a community of hope and of empowering change. As I look towards tomorrow and onward, it is clear that women are changing the world.

Be intentional with your healing journey. Create space to connect with your body. Be present and attune to your senses. Become familiar with the responses of your body. Connect, listen, trust, and honour your intuitive messages.

Allow your intuition to lead you. This is how you survive, and this is how you will thrive.

HOUA UTECH

Dedication - For my mothers,
Chao Lor & Ying Susan Yang -

Your bravery, your fight,
your survival, your plight.
You've come so far,
And now let us help carry this light.

ABOUT THE AUTHOR
HOUA UTECH

Houa Utech is a Trauma-Informed Coach who specializes in helping women heal from Betrayal Trauma, Covert Narcissistic Abuse, Complex PTSD, and Divorce/Post-separation Abuse to live an empowered life.

Before starting a coaching business, Houa spent several years as a social worker providing education, advocacy, and counseling to children, youth, women, and families. Houa is a member of the National Safe Parents Organization, a coalition of more than 100,000 survivor parents and concerned citizens in the United States advocating for evidence-based policies which put child safety and risks at the forefront of child custody decisions. Houa is a member and provides support to Wisconsin Safe Parents, a group committed to bringing awareness and change, at the state level, to protect children in child custody cases.

Houa enjoys living and learning alongside her four children. She also enjoys exploring through travel, art, photography, yoga, and meditation practices. Houa is available for 1:1 coaching.

You can reach Houa at:

Email: houautech@gmail.com

Website: www.houautech.com

Podcast: This Emboldened Life (Episodes to be released in October 2022)

facebook.com/houautech

instagram.com/houa_utech

8

LATHER, RINSE, REPEAT... UNTIL YOU DON'T.

JESSICA PARENTE

Dedicated to the memory of my dear friend, Karl Giese, who was the first to read this chapter in its entirety. My "dark twin flame" is less bright without you.

'WHO ARE YOU **REALLY** TALKING TO, JESS?'

Lather. Rinse. Repeat. – A life lesson I learned all too well. It took me years to figure out that the universe will keep giving you the same patterns and the same challenges. The same exact person but in another body. The same experiences and the same struggles but in different circumstances. It will keep giving you opportunities to learn the lessons you need to learn in order to heal, shift, grow, and improve. The lessons that will lead you to becoming the wonderful, amazing, thriving human being you are destined to be in this lifetime. The universe will keep giving you these opportunities time and time again. Trust me.

You will be given chances to act, react, or do things differently than you have in the past. Chances to break the cycles. To free yourself of generational curses. To liberate yourself from the chains that have held you down and held you back. But until you are ready to take off the blinders and pull back the veil, you're destined to repeat the same patterns and to get the same results. It's *lather, rinse, repeat*. Pay attention to the little signs. They are not coincidences. And when you're finally in a space to see these opportunities truly and clearly for what they are – chances to start fresh, chances to be reborn – Take these opportunities to rise out of the ashes as I have. It's *lather, rinse, repeat... until you don't*.

'Who are you **really** talking to, Jess?' asked my therapist.

I was relaying a conversation that was the start of the absolute worst argument I had with my narcissist. The argument began with me making a simple request. It quickly escalated to him telling me to *'shut the fuck up'* for hours as I was trying to respectfully explain how I felt. Like so many other times, it led to me begging and pleading for him to stop talking to me aggressively. Begging and pleading for him to just **try** and understand where I was coming from.

But this time, I didn't let it go. I didn't walk away. The flight, freeze, and fawn trauma responses of my childhood had now turned into a fight response in my adulthood. That argument led to him telling me that I deserved all the loneliness I felt as a child because I was *'so fucking annoying.'* And in the heat of that argument, and after months of escalating verbal and emotional abuse, I finally lost control.

Lather, Rinse, Repeat… Until You Don't.

That moment became the breaking point for me. In a reactive abuse response, I grabbed onto one of his belongings and chucked it across the room as I hysterically cried and cried. All of my inner child wounds were lit on fire when that hateful comment came spewing out of his mouth.

The pain was so intense. My head spun. *You're **not** good enough. You're **not** loved. You are **alone**. You're **not** even worth a decent conversation. You're **not** worth respect. Your feelings **don't** matter.* **YOU DON'T MATTER.** *You're annoying and you **deserved** every bit of pain you have **ever** felt in your entire life. It'd be better for everyone if you just fucking **died**.*

The argument eventually escalated from verbal abuse to physical abuse. That disagreement began with expressing my feelings, and it ended with injuries so severe that I was terrified to go to sleep that night for fear I'd stop breathing. That night was no different from so many others. My injuries didn't fully heal for three weeks. And the relationship didn't end until almost a month later.

My therapist interrupted my reverie, 'Jess…Who are you talking to?" My eyes welled up with tears. My throat tightened. My heart sank. *Don't even say it.*

'You're talking to your mother.'

In a prior session, I recounted an argument I had with my mother that resulted in her wrecking my bedroom. Frames, items… everything strewn about on the floor. My room was dismantled. Destroyed. Even now, I can't tell you what the fight was about. My only recollection was that my best, safest option was to leave and ride my bike to my Grandma Parente's house.

I wasn't allowed to cross one of the main roads that lead me there, but I didn't care about getting in trouble. The flight trauma response was in full force, and I left. I don't remember what happened that led us to that point. I don't remember what happened after. There are so many distressing memories related to my upbringing that don't seem real.

The number of times I question my reality greatly outweighs the memories that I know for sure occurred. I question myself constantly. I ask my therapist for reassurance as if she was there living it with me. But when it comes down to it, the memories are real to me, and that's all that matters.

My therapist was able to help me see that this argument with my narcissist was replaying a scenario with my mother from childhood. I was using different trauma responses (fight in adulthood, flight/freeze/fawn in childhood) yet getting the same shitty results and consequences. Nothing was getting solved. The situations and relationships weren't healed. *I wasn't healed.* It was the same shit but a different day.

Lather, rinse, repeat. This realization was ground-breaking for me. Earth-shattering. Eye-opening. Here I was, thirty years later, living out the same patterns of my childhood but hoping for different results.

The first time I ever heard the term *codependency* was in my mid-twenties. Despite desperately needing it my entire life, I didn't seek out mental health treatment until then. My incredible first therapist bluntly yet respectfully called me out on some of my *'crazy-making'* behaviors. Behaviors which stemmed from my upbringing and resulted in my overwhelming compulsion to control everything and everyone around me in order to feel safe. Reading *'Codependent No More'* felt like reading my autobiography. The irony of growing up believing I'm a special unique snowflake only to discover that there's literally a book describing me to a tee hit me hard. To realize that a huge bulk of my personality traits were merely codependent habits *masquerading* as personality traits. *If these habits had been learned and can be unlearned, and if I am not **actually** these things, then who the hell am I?!* That was the million-dollar question.

It's safe to say that growing up with a mother like mine wasn't easy. That's not to say that my mother is a bad person. She's not. She would give someone the shirt off her back. She is fun. She is friendly. She goes out of her way to help others. But she is a broken person. My mother battled with addiction for as long as I can remember. People like to think that children are naïve, but I assure you, they are not.

I knew from a very young age that something wasn't right in my home. I have fleeting memories that I question frequently. Memories of being in cars sitting outside her friends' homes waiting for her to come out. Memories of calling the bar looking for her. Memories of sitting by the window waiting for her headlights to come in the driveway so that I could run to bed and pretend I was asleep. Memories of all-night violent arguments between her and her boyfriend. Memories of hearing my brother cry in the next room during these fights. Memories of pulling him into my bed and then putting him back in his own before morning. Memories of being up all night feeling scared and unsafe yet going to school the next day and pretending like everything was fine.

My childhood was not the standard. There was nothing about it that was normal. I did my best to watch out for my little brother, but I was a child raising a child. I didn't know what the fuck I was doing. I did a lot of things wrong because I didn't know any better. I took my frustrations out on him because I didn't have any other avenues or outlets. I had no sense of emotional safety, even within the walls of my own home.

I became parentified at a very young age. And through my mom's battle with her demons, I created some of my own. I became a raging codependent. A perfectionistic, people-pleasing, academic, over-achieving, fixer, rescuer, martyr, depressed, anxious CONTROL FREAK HOT MESS EXPRESS. From the outside, I was a good girl, a top-performing student, a competitive dancer. A kind, caring, polite, respectful, fun human being. But on the inside, I was an absolute mess. *You're not good enough. You're not lovable. You're not worthy. You're not important. You're not safe. You're not deserving. You don't matter.* Even in a room full of people, people who I objectively **knew** loved me, I felt so fucking alone.

The vast majority of my life was spent going out into the world and attempting to **prove** my worth to others. *If I get all A's, if I do well at my dance competitions, if I let you cheat off of my schoolwork, if I work harder than everyone else, if I go to college to become a doctor, if I am a "good friend" (which sometimes means doing whatever you want even if I don't want to so that you won't be mad at me), if I let you use my body, if I go out of my way to help you even if I am running on empty, if I sacrifice my own happiness for yours, if I do all these things and more then you will* **have** *to know that I am good enough, RIGHT?!*

It was exhausting. I honestly don't know how I survived.

Lather, Rinse, Repeat… Until You Don't.

I was frozen in a never-ending cycle of doing everything for others, having shitty or non-existent boundaries, running myself into the ground, always saying *Yes*, and never saying *No*, letting people treat me however they saw fit, trying to be anything and everything to anyone and everyone even if they were showing up half-ass for me, forgiving others without ever receiving an apology… And even then, I'd STILL be right there waiting. Standing tall with all the fiercest loyalty. Absorbing copious amounts of negative energy with a great big smile on my face, a lump in my throat, and a gaping emptiness in my heart. All for the sake of proving that I was worth keeping around and that I was, in fact, good enough. Even if it was at the expense of my own dignity, boundaries, and self-respect.

Those unhealed inner child wounds remained for so many years, unknowingly leading me from one toxic friendship, relationship, and situation to the next. With every shitty ending of those relationships was the reiteration and validation of those words: *You're not good enough. You're not lovable. You're not worthy.*

You're not important. You're not safe. You're not deserving. You don't matter. There are so many people who are wounded little children walking around in grown-up bodies, and I most definitely felt like the queen of them.

Deciding to pull the trigger on going to therapy didn't happen by accident. Despite living a *secretly* depressed, anxious, and miserable-ass existence for most of my life, it took losing someone I loved in my mid-twenties to **finally** light that fire under my ass.

Losing him validated those inner child wounds, and I was desperate. I catapulted myself into the first (but definitely not the last) segment of my self-healing journey. *I will fix myself so that he loves me. I will get better so that I am not "too much." I will show him that I am dedicated. Getting him back will mean that I really am loveable, good enough, and worth it. So I will get him back even if it kills me!*

The funny thing is, I did start to get better, and I did get him back. I stopped therapy, and we spent ten amazing, awful, happy, sad, and obviously very complex years together. He was the safest, most stable romantic relationship and friendship of my life thus far. But after a few years, something didn't click quite right. We were amazing companions, the best of friends, a fun couple to be around, but *something* was missing.

That amazing man, along with the safety and security of that relationship, masked whatever inner child wounds were left gaping and bleeding under the codependent habits that remained. It cushioned me. It kept those wounds nice and hidden. Catered to with a cocktail and a cuddle. Despite all of my best efforts, the talk therapy, couple's therapy, self-help books, forcing and trying, and trying and forcing, my inner child wounds lived on. My mind felt better - more clear and rational, but my body was still off. I *thought* better, but I didn't *feel* better. I was *somewhat* healed but not *entirely* healed.

We blamed everything under the sun for the disconnect: my depression, my grief, my school, his job, my job, family dying, friends dying, stress, lack of time, lack of effort. We tried so hard to rationalize and make sense of it all. But no matter how hard we tried, that *'almost there but not quite'* feeling we had for years of the relationship, that feeling he referred to as me

Lather, Rinse, Repeat… Until You Don't.

'opening the door so far and then slamming it in his face,' and that emotional wall that left me so fucking frustrated with myself because I **loved** this man remained. I saw him for all the wonderful that he was so *why couldn't I let myself love him the way he deserved?*

The self-blame and self-hatred grew as I continued to wrack my brain, trying desperately to figure out what the fuck was wrong with me. But despite my best efforts, we remained stuck. Eventually, that feeling we tried so hard to ignore for years led us to making the most difficult, heart-wrenching and selfless choice we could… and let each other go.

Our separation was immensely painful, scary, and tragic. There are still days where I will tear up over missing our home, our cats, our couch, or our fun times together. But most of all, I just miss my friend. I truly hope that he is living the happy, fulfilling, love and lust-filled life that I always knew he deserved. A life that I so desperately wanted to give him but couldn't. It has taken a lot of time, self-reflection, learning, and extremely painful experiences to finally understand **exactly** what stood in our way – And that was the wiring of my nervous system.

See, when you grow up in an environment like the one I did, where you are constantly walking on eggshells, where you don't know what to expect next, your nervous system becomes conditioned for this. It becomes primed for the highs and lows. I never knew what mood my mom would be in. What type of fight my brother and I would get into. What kind of drama would rear its ugly head. What bullshit argument her Nazi boyfriend was going to start and then continue into the wee hours of the night. What things would be broken, shattered, or dismantled during said argument. How much sleep I would get, **if any**.

I was constantly on edge, anticipating any and all situations that might occur next. I would think of every single possibility so I would know exactly how to react when it happened. It was the only way that I felt some sort of half-ass semblance of safety. It was constant fight or flight.

That conditioning becomes the norm for your nervous system. Your nervous system feeds off it. And as fucked up as it is, you don't feel alive without it. My nervous system wasn't primed for the safety and security of my ex because it had never experienced safety and security before. It didn't know how to exist in the calm because it didn't know what the hell *calm* was. My nervous system wasn't primed for calm. It was primed for chaos... Aaaaand in walks the narcissist.

Relationships with a narcissist start like every other relationship with every other narcissist. Their dating strategies are pulled straight from their subconscious playbook. Once you're finally outside of the fog and can see things for what they are, it's not even that good of a fucking playbook. Love-bombing. Future-promising. Mirroring your behaviors and everything that you like, want, and value in life so that you think you've finally found your person. Every aspect of the relationship moves so fast. As if you're caught up in some incredible love tornado. *This. This excitement. This passion. This high. This is what has been missing. This **has** to be it. This is what all that pain was for. It was leading me exactly where I should be.* But if you ask any survivor, it's all the same.

Lather, Rinse, Repeat... Until You Don't.

My experience *was* leading me exactly where I should be. Just never in the way I had originally imagined.

During the *love-bombing phase*, the oxytocin, serotonin, and dopamine flooded my brain so heavily and so frequently that I couldn't see straight. It felt amazing. But I'd be lying if I said my gut wasn't telling me something was off within the first couple weeks. I wasn't comfortable with how quickly things were moving, so I tried to put down boundaries. But I was a codependent with shitty boundaries, so I let things go. I began to notice that even communicating the most nonchalant feeling turned into a major disagreement. That's when my rational brain would kick in and stifle my gut, though it was not for my benefit. If there's one thing I've learned in life, it's that not trusting your gut is a recipe for disaster.

Well, Jess, you do over-communicate. Maybe you need to keep your thoughts and feelings to yourself sometimes. Not everyone communicates the way your ex did. You need to learn how other people operate. This is what dating is like. Maybe you need to pick and choose your battles. Maybe you are asking too much.

Gut silenced. Boundary violated. Easy-peasy. Moving on.

Ignoring my gut became second-nature. I shut her down as frequently as I did in childhood. I allowed things to happen to me and around me that I felt were not okay. And no matter how many other situations

like this happened, even when they were happening daily, I rationalized. In my career, rationalizing, over-analyzing, and intellectualizing are all strengths. They prevent me from internalizing my client's emotional energy even when it's directed at me. They help me understand the **why** behind behaviors so that I can best guide my clients towards recovery. But as a girlfriend and a victim of narcissistic abuse, rationalization does nothing but keep you chained, trapped, and questioning yourself to the point of insanity.

I knew something was off within the first couple weeks, yet I stayed. I was already trauma-bonded. And with every push back that came from him, I tried harder. I tried to compromise. I tried to choose my battles. I tried to understand where he was coming from even if it was at the expense of my own feelings. I stuffed things down. I got mocked for *'things always triggering me.'* I distinctly remember saying more than a dozen times, *'Sometimes being around you reminds me of being around my mom.'* If this alone wasn't a red flag staring me right in the fucking face, I don't know what was. But still, I pushed forward.

Walking on eggshells. Stuffing my feelings and thoughts down. Anticipating every reaction but usually getting an aggressive one. Getting the silent treatment. Feeling guilty for things that weren't my fault. Feeling guilty for having a feeling, an opinion, a thought or something to say. Feeling guilty for being me. Feeling guilty for being alive.

Feeling guilty all day, every day.

I was reliving my traumatic childhood experiences any time I tried to communicate anything. It never felt

safe. It never felt comfortable. But it felt *familiar*. Constant fight or flight. *Lather, rinse, repeat.*

Victims often talk about a *'turning point'* where the narcissist switches from idolizing you to hating you. The covert abuse I experienced was more of a slow insidious burn. Rationalization began to lose its luster. The manipulation, blame-shifting, and

Lather, Rinse, Repeat... Until You Don't.

gaslighting all intensified over time. The gaming was a non-stop issue. The drinking became a very apparent pain point and a bigger problem than I ever imagined.

What's funny is, for my entire life, I promised myself that I would **NEVER** choose to live in an environment similar to the one I grew up in. And what did I do? I literally and semi-willingly created the environment that I grew up in. Fully equipped with my adult version of Dr. Jekyll & Mr. Hyde. Once again, I had no sense of emotional safety, even within the walls of my own home.

Lather, rinse, repeat.

Amongst the madness, there were still happy moments and fun times. Things they refer to as *breadcrumbs of love*. The *breadcrumbs* would be tossed right before I hit my breaking points, and I would be satiated for a second. But it was never too long before the lows took over again. And the lows were LOW.

Many days, I felt completely and utterly depleted. But my nervous system was THRIVING. High. Low. High. Low. This is what it was conditioned for. It felt alive in the addiction to the chaos. But slowly, I lost everything. Myself, my sanity, my sense of reality, my will to live. I was a shell of the person I used to be.

At this point, I had to walk away, right?! NOPE. In typical codependent fashion, I tried harder. I tried to manifest any *turning point* towards us getting better so that I had hope for something. Because without hope, I had nothing left. *I'll prove that I can make this work. I'll prove to him that I wasn't lying when I said I loved him, cared about him, and accepted him for who he is. I'll prove* *that my love is unconditional. I'll prove that I will be here through the good and the bad. Even if the bad is **really** bad.*

This is exactly why codependents and narcissists are magnets for each other. Codependents will give, give, give until they have less-than-nothing left. And the narcissist will take, take, take. Take it all and then some just because they feel entitled to it. Then, as you are anorexic and starving from giving them every piece of you that you possibly have to offer, they have the balls to ask for more.

The night before he left, I had one of the longest and worst panic attacks I had experienced in years. In the middle of the night, I found him passed out on the loveseat. I hugged him tightly while slobbering tears, boogers, and spit all over him. I kept repeating the phrases, *'You're going to die doing what you're doing. I want to save you, but I can't. I have to let you go. I want to save you, but I can't save you no matter how hard I try or how much I want to.'* Over, and over, and over again like a bad broken record.

The hopelessness and helplessness that I felt my entire life collectively suffocated me and weighed me down in that exact moment. I was wrapped up in a dark cloud of desperation that I could not escape. And in my head, I heard my therapist's words.

*'Who are you **really** talking to, Jess?'*

I thought that night and the day that followed were as low as it could get. Unfortunately for me, my ROCK-rock bottom had yet to come. The *discard phase* came to fruition only a few weeks later when he inevitably found his first new supply. I was completely devastated. The intrusive suicidal thoughts that plagued my brain since I was nine years old were at an all-time high. The depth of that sadness is something that I can't even put into words. For months, I didn't eat, I didn't sleep, I didn't leave my house. I didn't do much other than work, lay on my couch, and go through the motions like a drugged-out zombie. I was slowly waiting for death to take me. Hoping for it, actually. My focus was on surviving. And I was barely doing that.

But during that time, I also educated myself. I listened to podcasts, I watched documentaries, I read survivor stories. I reflected back on my life and on every situation and repeated situation that had led me to that point. *How long are you going to let this go on, Jess? How many similar situations need to happen before you* **finally** *get it? You can clearly see WHY he was brought to you, can't you? You weren't learning any other way!*

The narcissist was the catalyst for finally healing the inner child wounds that plagued me for so long. The universe used this relationship to shove those patterns of repeated trauma into my face and so far down my throat that there was NO POSSIBLE WAY I could continue to ignore them. Once and for all, I was sick and tired of being sick and tired. Then, after a few months, and with the help of my family of friends, my kittens, my therapist, Caroline, the serendipity of life, and myself... I slowly started to crawl out of that hole.

To say my life is completely different since starting my self-healing journey is an understatement. To say *I* am completely different is an understatement. My life is full of smiles, peace, love, open communication, compassion, validation, advocating for myself, kitty snuggles, hugs, concerts (oh, so many concerts!), travel, opportunity, clarity, connection, belly-laughs, healing, self-compassion, self-love, self-worth, trusting my gut, better boundaries, productive days, lazy days, good days, bad days, and everything in between.

I'm not going to pretend like every day is a good day or that I don't still struggle because I do. I'm not going to act like the trauma-bond doesn't kick in and make me miss certain aspects of relationships that are no longer serving me because it does. But even on the bad days, I am living my life intentionally and genuinely. I make my own decisions. Not the trauma. Not the inner child wounds. **ME**. I am doing the hard somatic work necessary to rewire my nervous system and to heal those inner child wounds once and for all.

Slowly but surely, I am finding myself again, and the universe is responding in monumental fashion. The number of good things that have come into my life since I've made the conscious choice to break the cycle and rise out of the ashes is astronomical. It's honestly surreal. And I am not alone. There are so many of us *'wounded little children in adult bodies'* that are healing. The generational trauma breakers. The abuse survivors. The real-life superheroes. The universe is connecting us, and THAT. IS. POWERFUL.

It's ugly, and it's painful, and it's scary to try something different. To heal. To shift. To break free of your past. To break free of the past that came long before you and that you didn't sign up for. To break free of *yourself*. But it's just as ugly, and painful, and scary to stay stuck and to remain comfortable in the discomfort for the rest of your life.

Lather, Rinse, Repeat… Until You Don't.

So, pay attention to the patterns of your life. They aren't happening by accident.

The narcissist *was* leading me exactly where I am meant to be. Because through the depths of that indescribable pain, I was able to rise stronger, more determined, and more resilient than ever. It was *lather, rinse, repeat…* until I didn't.

ABOUT THE AUTHOR
JESSICA PARENTE

Jessica Parente is a Psychiatric Mental Health Nurse Practitioner and a Trauma-Informed Coach. Her unique skill set and approach to treatment fosters an environment for healing via a combination of symptom management and root-cause resolution.

Before her current endeavors, Jess spent five years as a Pediatric Oncology Nurse at Children's Hospital of Pittsburgh. She also worked as a Milieu Therapist at various Pittsburgh-based mental health facilities prior to pursuing her career in nursing.

Currently, Jessica uses her vast work experience and training to help clients live authentic and fulfilling lives, free of generational traumas and codependency.

Jess enjoys traveling, live music, and spending quality time with her friends and her two cats, *Hiro* and *Haru*.

Jessica will be available for one-to-one telehealth-based medication management and/or trauma-healing in various independent practice states across the US.

You can reach Jess at:

Email - info@generationaljess.com

Website - www.generationaljess.com

9

THE GIRL FROM THE WRONG SIDE OF THE RIVER

JOANNE FISHER

To the woman wherever you may be.

Forty-two years of learning has taught me without doubt that women are warriors. From observing my grandmother, my mother, my daughters, my friends and colleagues; the challenges we face are far beyond anything we are prepared or ever given credit for. Our bodies and minds go through so much yet we carry on. Relentlessly, we pick ourselves up and just keep moving forward and for that I SALUTE YOU.

Looking through my eyes is a gift. I can finally say that I am proud of who I have become and each step I took that got me here. I am wiser and stronger than I ever thought possible, something I thank myself for daily.

If I told you that every day felt full of love and admiration for myself though, I would be lying. The work on yourself never stops, it continues and will always be a part of my life but I am now able to say with honesty and certainty that I love the woman I am today and am becoming. She is brave, she leads from the heart, and she believes in her worthiness. But, that was not always the case.

I am able to look back at myself and smile at the thought of what I once was. This didn't always feel possible but each day is a step towards mastering the woman I will become, the woman who evolves as each new phase of life passes her by.

Life is now intentional. It's not just something that happens to me. I have chosen what I want my life to look like and every single day I take conscious courageous steps towards achieving it, like writing this chapter for instance, it is all a part of the healing process, positive forward action every single day in despite of the fear. Hoping and wishing for the life you desire is just not enough - as they say, *"a wish written down becomes a plan"* and a plan gives you a strategy to move towards your goals when you remain in control and positive.

As a lawyer I believed my path was obvious. I would qualify, get a job and work that job until retirement all the while competing to be the best in a room full of other lawyers who were all doing exactly the same - competing to be the best. I remember being asked by an old in a room full of other lawyers – *'who here sees themselves as a disruptor?'* I was among two or three who were brave enough to raise their hands. His response was to politely remind us that we were not the disruptors but the business he had developed *'for us'* was indeed disrupting the market and we were part of the process by following him.

I remember in that moment knowing that this was not where I was supposed to be.

I now run an online legal consultancy disrupting and breaking the norms of how entrepreneurs access legal services, taking away the fear and allowing them to feel safe as they scale their businesses. I no longer just fit in the box - I am a best-selling author and my business gives me the freedom I have always craved and as I sit at a beautiful desk in a beautiful home serving women who inspire me every single day to do and be better I am so full of gratitude, I get to choose when I work and when I will make memo- ries with my four beautiful children and that to me is more success than I ever dreamed possible. The future is exciting.

I couldn't ever have imagined that this would be my life now.

I used to believe that love was always going to be a battle, that love would hurt and happiness wasn't really meant for someone like me. My belief was that life was always going to be difficult and that as long as someone didn't leave me it really didn't matter how they treated me because if they were willing to stay despite the bad then that must have meant that they really loved me, unconditionally and without question. And, for that I should be grateful.

I would find ways of seeing the good in people no matter how bad it got and in the worst moments I always found a way to blame myself, that somehow, some way I had done something wrong that caused their reaction to me. That I was somehow damaged and deserved the way I was treated.

As long I was doing what I *should* be doing and building the life I had planned out in my head, the career, the baby, the house, the wedding, the group of friends then I was ok with the treatment I received along the way. As long as I didn't rock the boat too much, I was fine to just keep moving forward and brushing the *bad* under the carpet because I saw myself as lucky for breaking away from the constraints of my childhood.

My focus was all wrong. I attached no value to myself and relied totally on external validation. Provided what could be seen from the outside looked fine that was enough. I strived to be the best in everything I did because the more I could achieve and show materially then the less I had to look inside and actually deal with what I really thought about myself. When I think back at how I let so much go in my younger years because I didn't want to be judged or rejected I feel so sad for that girl and how she felt about herself.

Forgiving yourself is tough, its a process that you need to commit to. That younger version of me didn't know why she was fighting so hard, she didn't understand why she would let others walk all over her until she reached the very limits of her being only then to let out a cry for help but quickly retreat because to actually follow through and stand up for herself and what she believed in was just too scary. I resented her for so long for causing trouble, being dramatic, thinking too much of herself and not being able to just '*be happy*' like everyone else.

I see now that she was afraid. She was afraid of judgment, rejection, power, imperfection, she was afraid of everything so she built a wall to protect herself from all of that pain and fear. A wall so strong that from the outside looking in she was invincible and could never be powerless. Her fortress was her strength.

The truth is I held no power back then. I was easily led, ached to be liked, jumped into everything feet first and thought about it later, I needed people's validation so much so that I would be whoever they wanted me to be. If I was with people who I grew up with I was the *council estate girl*, if I was with work colleagues I was the *middle class lawyer*, if I was at a party I was the one who *partied the hardest*, wherever you put me I would adapt like a chameleon and be exactly whoever they wanted me to be, because as long as I was liked it stopped me from feeling the unworthiness, it stopped me from feeling like the little girl from the wrong side of the river.

I grew up on one of the worst council estates in the county. A place where police, drugs, fighting, alcohol and unemployment were the norm. My father had left when I was just two years old and while he dipped in and out for a while, before long he was just a man who visited every few years, the first man who ever broke my heart. I vividly remember sitting for hours at the bottom of our staircase on a Saturday morning in my little red duffle coat, I can't have been older than six years old, refusing to move from that step and accept that he wasn't coming to pick me up. I also remember feeling my mother's sadness.

After that my mum and nan raised me together, my nan's house was my safety, and I would stay there as often as I could to feel the calm safety net that she offered me.

The chaos of my childhood continued well into my teens, there was an air of uncertainty that I could never quite put my finger on, a constant subconscious fear that I just could never quite shift.

I was sent to a *good school* outside of the area where I lived because my mum wanted the best for me. Despite my sometimes unstable home life where alcohol, parties, fighting and arguments were never too far away, she stayed strong and kept trying to give us the best but on times it was out of control.

Going to the *good school*, seemed like it was the best option for me, but what it actually meant was that that I never really fitted in anywhere. I was the girl from the rough council estate, with the dark skin who had the free school dinners - a prime target for cruel kids and on the estate where I lived

I was the *good girl* who went to the *posh school* and so was never quite like everyone else. What that meant was that in both worlds I never really felt like I connected with friends. By the time I went to comprehensive school the bullying where I lived ramped up. I remember the fear going out and feeling constantly under threat from the cooler *hard girls*, girls who would wait across the street outside my house and chase me until I was too tired to run anymore. Who would then hit me and tell me how pathetic I was. Girls who would glare at me as I tried to fit in letting me know that I was in their sights. I found it so much easier to connect with boys or that was what I told myself for a very long time. That stage of my life exasperated my fear of everything, and I quickly relied on a boyfriend and his group of friends to keep me *safe*.

By the time I left home at seventeen I had mastered the art of looking like I had it all together; my fortress was strong and I refused to let the fears, self-doubt, unworthiness, shame and guilt from ever showing up in public. They remained well and truly locked down and I was going to change my life no matter what. I put myself through university while I worked full time to fund my rent and my lifestyle. Failing was just simply never going to be an option.

At the age of nineteen I met my first husband, the boy from the right side of the river. He was everything and more I had planned for my future, his love was passionate, he held nothing back and for the first time in my life there was no doubt that he wanted me and was never going to leave. Within three months we were living together, within a year we had bought our first house, I was finally living my dream and from the outside I had everything a girl could want, especially a girl looking for validation from anywhere other than inside herself yet behind the scenes life was already volatile.

The relationship lasted for ten years and gave me my first child but what it took from me was a whole lot more.

The perfect romance, the perfect man, the perfect wedding, the perfect dress, the perfect home, the perfect child but in reality, a toxic mix of anger, jealousy and pain. Friends would tell me that our relationship was passionate and label us both as being *'just as bad as one another'* all the while this so-called love was nothing short of destroying me.

I allowed the relationship to tap into every conscious and unconscious belief about myself. I felt like nothing again and believed that the breakdown of the marriage was all my own doing because I was not deserving, because I just couldn't be happy, because I was unworthy and because I couldn't make him love me more, because I was the scum from the wrong side of the river.

The marriage ended when my daughter was a little over one because then it was no longer just about me, I couldn't hide behind a facade anymore of what life looked like on the outside. I was fooling no one but myself by this point and the arguments and volatility were getting worse. I had to think about the impact it would have on her. That was a power I had never experienced before, something new inside me had ignited, a furness that was growing and an unwavering need to protect her from pain. Now it was about her.

I went away to the South of France with my closest friends and as I sat and listened to the stories of their marriages and the love that was so obviously there, I knew right then that it was the last holiday I would spend questioning myself. I knew I wanted out and I came home and immediately communicated it was the end, I had said it so many times before but somehow this felt different, and we both knew it.

The split was painful, as painful as the years before I had spent questioning why things had got so bad and eventually I took my daughter into rented accommodation, and we started again.

Over the years that followed I found myself in a constant spiral of rows with my ex-husband, tentatively dating and partying as hard as I could to avoid actually dealing with what was going on inside. I finally met someone new who I slowly started to see a future with until the insecure, unworthy girl reared her head again.

I was a magnet to men who wanted to save me, it was almost as if they could see the vulnerability a mile off. The love was overwhelming, I was well and truly love bombed with proposals despite me still being married, daily declarations of love with gifts left on my car and popping into my house while I slept at night to make sure I was safe, he made me feel like the only woman on earth - a sure fire way to get into the head of someone who is so full of self-doubt. Someone who so desperately wanted to show the world that she was not just the girl who kept messing up.

To say that this relationship ended badly is an understatement. It was as if the pain from the breakdown of my marriage that I had kept in check for so long and the pain of the way this was ending all came at once. It left me torn open and the pain was insurmountable. I was powerless to him and had no fight left in me after over ten years of battling with my ex so I retreated and allowed shame and failure to wash over me once again.

I had allowed myself to dream that this was my new beginning, that the life I had so desperately wished for was in reach, that maybe I would have more children and after three miscarriages since the birth of my first daughter, I knew I just needed to heal.

I focused inward, concentrated on my daughter and my career and finally years later I met someone else. I felt like a new woman, I believed I had done the work on myself, I was no longer searching for external validation, I was doing ok, or so I thought.

What I now know is that I had once again cleverly managed to suppress years and years of wounds from abandonment, unworthiness, shame and guilt and as a result my fortress was stronger and higher than it had ever been. I continued to only allow people to see the parts I felt safe in sharing.

In this new relationship, I went on to have three children, a daughter just three years in and then a beautiful surprise in 2018 when I fell pregnant with twins. By that time, I was running my own legal practice and had an office on my local high street with three amazing women supporting me, I was finally on my way to achieving the life I had so desperately yearned for and it was on my terms. It was right there in touching distance, I just needed to push a little bit harder to reach it but then it all came crashing down.

The pregnancy was tough, I had severe morning sickness for the first five months and then complication after complication. I felt like I was fading and out of fear and panic just a month before the twins were born, I decided to let go of my staff and close down my business. I felt I had no choice as we were just not sure what the next few months would hold. I see now I hit the self destruct button yet again.

The pregnancy in medical terms was something known as *monochorionic diamniotic twins*, we were very high risk as the babies were sharing one placenta and one gestational sack and we were continually told to prepare for the worst. As the weeks passed I could feel the doubt and unworthiness setting in again. To my mind I was once again failing, happiness was not meant for me.

The more I felt like I was failing, the more my past *failures* returned to haunt me.

In a *moment* it all changed. Everything in my life had been building to *that moment*. A *moment* that would eventually bring me back to me, the real me, my true self I just didn't quite know it yet.

In that *moment*, when I felt all was lost, I turned my head and there she was my beautiful first born sat at the end of the kitchen table watching me. The look of fear in her eyes shook me.

As I looked into her eyes, I felt my partner's arms firmly holding my waist from where he had wrestled the foil packet of tablets from my hands and me away from the kitchen worktops.

In the seconds before I had needed it all to stop, I needed the world to go away, I wanted it all to be over. The fear, the guilt, the anxiety and the absolute gut-wrenching shame. I wanted it all to just go away.

I didn't recognise myself, a woman who couldn't control the panic and anger raging through her.

My body was hot and wet and my heart was still racing when her eyes met mine. I had looked into those big brown eyes for over twelve years but somehow, they looked different and in that *moment* I felt I had changed her forever. There was a sadness I hadn't seen before and I feared it went deep, so deep that she would never recover.

Spectators in those *moments* feel so helpless and in the brief moments of clarity that I had, I knew that I was hurting them all and the guilt and shame that came with that became too much.

Removing myself from the situation would protect them all from the pain of seeing me become more fragile and those thoughts were getting louder and louder in my head. *Surely, they were better off without me?* And then my mind would be quiet.

Feeling a pain so deep that you just can't explain, can't let go of and don't know how to process was the most frightening experience of my life. To feel fear and guilt and yet feel so blessed and full of love is torturous. To cry and to scream until your eyes and throat are raw and you can't cry and scream anymore had been tough on us all but nothing like the point I reached on that particular night.

As I relive this moment it now feels like it was someone else. That girl was not me... but who was she and where did she come from - I feared she was here to stay? Little did I know how much power she held and how much I really needed her. She had always been there, she was just buried deep within waiting for the right *moment* to show herself.

I sat with my knees hugged so tightly into my chest sobbing in the corner, all I could hear was the doctors soft words, *'You're going to be ok Joanne, you're ok, what you're trying to do right now is tough, do you still feel like you want to harm yourself?'*

That night was just one in a long line of days since I had given birth to the twins where I had sobbed and screamed and felt totally useless as I desperately tried to breast feed two tiny babies who weren't out of the woods yet, constantly worrying that the worst was going to happen but that night the guilt and overwhelm became too much to bear and I knew, I 100% absolutely knew they would all be better off without me.

Sweat poured from every part of my body, I felt like I was on fire with hormones and anger just raging through me, my tears hadn't stopped for weeks, every time I looked at the babies, I felt overwhelmed with a feeling of uselessness, who was I kidding thinking that I could do this, that I deserved them? What kind of a mother cant be strong for her babies?

My weight was down to just seven and a half stone, and I was becoming thinner and thinner by the day, running on adrenaline alone, but to the outside world I was doing great and was constantly praised for bouncing back so quickly after having my beautiful babies. I made sure that's what they saw just as I always had. Little did they know that on the inside I was slowly shutting down and that the guilt and shame that I was experiencing was all becoming too much to bear.

I don't recall what led to that exact *moment* on that exact day, but I do remember so vividly the pain, it was all too much, too much to take and I just couldn't make the self-destructive continual voices in my head just go away. I remember running to the kitchen and shouting *'I just can't do this anymore, I need it to stop'*.

The fear in my child's face will be fixed in my brain forever, it's an image that hits me every now and then - it used to remind me of what a terrible mother I was, but now it is an image reminding me of how far I have come and my commitment to do better. My first born beautiful twelve-year-old girl watched on as her mum broke right in front of her eyes.

I cried I just want to end it, *'I can't do it anymore'*. My partner's arms were hugged around my waist as the realisation dawned on him of what I was about to do, things were bad, but this was a whole other level. He held me so tightly - I hated him, in that moment, I hated everything and everyone ...but really I just hated myself.

He pulled the pills from my hands and shouted at me to pull myself together he then called the doctor. I really hated him for that. I needed to be seen.

The reality of what was going on and the shame that I felt along- side it had consumed me, my frail tiny breastfeeding twins who were barely gaining weight under daily scrutiny and judgement or so I felt of the midwives visits meant I finally broke, every part of who I knew myself to be had disappeared and now I was failing yet again.

The guilt as I sat questioning everything about myself, my ability as a mother, my career, wishing that life hadn't become so tough, wishing I wasn't so tired, so damaged, wishing my babies would just sleep for two minutes longer to stop the constant burning sensation in my eyes and the constant sadness yet I was being reminded daily of how lucky and blessed I was.

That day everything changed, but now I see it was the beginning of finding my way back to me, the real me.

What was quickly labelled as post-natal depression was the trigger for real change. A change that went way back to my roots. It was time to break free from the fortress and become the woman I was meant to be without shame, guilt, frustration, that constant inner critic telling me *'I'm no good'* and the anxiety so debilitating that some days I would just walk relentlessly around the house waiting for the bad thing to happen.

It was time to break the cycle and set myself free. Because that's the truth isn't it, subconsciously we create our reality, what we see and feel we become, and I had done that for so long. When I finally accepted that the power was all within me, that it was all in my control my whole world changed.

You see this isn't a sad story of a woman wronged it is a story of hope that we can all change the narrative because it really is that simple that when you hit rock bottom there is only one way to go and that is back up.

One tiny step at a time you can rebuild. You can rebuild a life by design, you can have the life you want, you do not need to be a product of your circumstances, you get to choose.

What I quickly learnt was that my vulnerability had left me exposed to broken people, not bad people. I attracted those people into my life and then took on the burden of the failures like a badge of honour, it was almost addictive. I didn't value myself and the belief that I was unlovable and unworthy was programmed into me from that very moment I sat on that staircase and waited and waited. My relationship with men was never going be the dream I had wished for because I believed love was hard and chaotic and that rejection meant I was not good enough, so I would do all I could to maintain the *status quo of chaos* but somehow try to prevent the rejection. The result a never-ending cycle of pain.

To hold onto the past and put the blame on other serves no one, it only deprives you of your peace of mind. And peace to me is real success. To wake up feeling at ease and knowing that while my life may still have twists and turns that I now have the self- awareness to master my own thoughts is everything.

Healing is an ongoing process but now when I see parts of me like anger, frustration, the awful destructive inner critic or even anxiety creeping in I am able to get curious and ask '*Why am I feeling like that?* In those moments I now see that I am not being myself and it's that wounded little girl who didn't feel good enough all those years ago and her little army of protectors building her a fortress to make sure she doesn't feel pain showing up again. With that awareness I am able to move quickly through those feelings with love and see a situation now for what it really is. Because now as a forty-two year old woman with four children I am safe, I am worthy and I am in control - AND SO ARE YOU.

For a while medication was essential to calm my mind, in those dark moments especially quietening the thoughts was so important. I then dived into books, self-care and podcasts and eventually connected with experts to learn ways to change the way I thought. It takes a real commitment and positive intentional action every single day to develop practices that really help you move the needle in your life forward.

For me understanding was pivotal because when you really know yourself and understand why you react the way you do that when you truly become the master of your thoughts and can start to create a life by choice. I've also created daily habits like journaling, yoga, meditation and use affirmations so that I have a daily reminder of who I am, what the future holds and how far I have come.

Changing your life doesn't happen by chance.

I am not a counsellor or a therapist and I can't coach you back to wellbeing, but what I hope for you from this chapter is that whoever you are and wherever you come from that you find a sense of belonging, a knowing that you are not alone and that you are worthy of everything and more, it's yours for the taking, you just need to believe it and take intentional action to move toward it.

Know that whatever the challenge, you have the power to change the narrative, you can always escape and build a new life, you can change your frequency and learn strategies to avoid being a magnet for the broken. We can't change everyone but we most definitely can change ourselves, one woman at a time and with that, I whole heartedly believe we will eventually change the world.

It doesn't matter where we're from, or how we started or even what we've been through, we all have the right to feel safe. To never feel like we need to fight for our own security.

That's my mission. To pathe the way for women to stop feeling like they're always fighting to get back up, and to stop feeling a need to prove themselves over and over again. We don't need to take a back seat and let others shine.

ABOUT THE AUTHOR
JOANNE FISHER

We can have all that we want.

We can be all we ever wanted to be. We can be more.

We may need to push through obstacles and barriers to make that happen, but when we feel supported, protected, and heard that no longer feels as scary, or intimidating.

I've been there, seen it, and lived it. I fought to prove myself as a lawyer in the corporate world for 20 years, never really fitting in and being forced into a box that just wasn't me. And since leaving that world I've met and worked with so many incredible entrepreneurs who feel those same feelings and hold themselves back because they've been pushed down in the past.

The community of female entrepreneurs online inspires me every single day. It's my favourite part of what I do and helping women to harness and share their talent fulfils me like the corporate world never could.

Because when you have the right processes, contracts and documents you will feel ready to put yourself out there. Ready to push through the fear and create the life you want, setting you up for success like never before.

When you feel safe and protected, anything is possible. www.joannefisherlaw.co.uk

10

THE SILENT SCREAMS WITHIN

KIM PONTARELLI

If someone told me that my life would be what it is today, I would have never believed that I would be living a vibrant, exciting, fulfilled life full of love, excitement, stability, and humor. I am remarried to the most caring, loving, funny, passionate man who loves me with his whole being and treats me with the respect that I finally truly believe I deserve.

We are true partners who communicate respectfully. We love living life together, whether we are traveling or just staying in watching TV. We are both wild about each other. I know women who were previously in toxic relationships and became addicted to the highs and lows and think that anyone else will be dull and boring. That is not the case. I can assure you. My new life is fabulous. It's everything I have ever dreamt a relationship could be.

We both know it's the little things that matter day in and day out. To find a man who loves me so completely and unconditionally, I had to first love myself. I know this is not what you want to hear especially if you are currently in the state, I was previously in. I would roll my eyes and hate hearing this in the past. Loving yourself and not settling in any area of your life is the greatest truth and gift you can give yourself.

I have also had the opportunity to invest in many businesses and to start earning my own income with my coaching business. I love what I do as it gives me such meaning and purpose. I thought that I could never earn my own money and now I see that I'm a confident, intelligent woman capable of being a savvy business woman. I have had success with real estate transactions and am a partner in many thriving businesses. I had no experience in anything like this before and I'm so proud of where I am today. I'm still learning but I'm more confident with each day.

I have a beautiful relationship with my children. I thought my divorce would ruin my relationship with them. However, they have a mom who can be herself, and once they saw the real me without being a nervous wreck, walking on eggshells they saw my true essence. They love me for the person I am. We have deep, meaningful discussions and silly ones too. They have helped get me to the other side and are kind wonderful souls. I would say my relationship with them is even better.

I used to be walked all over and taken advantage of. I would give my kindness to everyone. Many didn't deserve it. I was the kind of person that would know I was right but take blame in every area of my life. I would walk into a chair, for God's sake, and apologize. I now set boundaries and speak my mind. I don't let things fester, and I refuse to minimize myself any longer.

How did I start this path to a healing journey? Notice: I didn't say healed. To me, healing is the same as being healthy. I never say I am on a diet. I say it's a lifestyle. I now approach my healing in the same manner.

Take for example this chapter, it is not what I originally planned. I had to tweak it for legal reasons. Because of my journey and with nervous system flexibility, I was able to calmly change it and provide you with what I hope is meaningful, authentic and a helpful chapter. Most of all I hope I touch your soul!

If this had happened in the past, I would have been crying, upset and all of my protector parts and voices would have strongly emerged, causing me to back out of the entire project. Those voices that have been in my head since about 3 years old, would call out to me. They would say things such as, "you can't do this, you are stupid, you always fail, no one cares what you have to say. You will look so dumb and be a failure." Just a short time ago I was not aware that many of us have these inner critic voices in our head, there to sabotage us.

In my healing journey, and later through my certification with the angel Caroline Strawson, I have learned that these are protector parts. With my clients I regularly use *Internal Family Systems Therapy* (IFS). This therapy has clients name and become familiar with these unwanted parts instead of pushing them down, which causes them to only further bubble up.

My clients see that these parts do not define them, but rather are just a part of them. I have named my ugly inner critic *Hilda*! These parts actually protect us from something our nervous system perceives as even worse than these critical voices. I now use many modalities with my clients to really take a deep dive into where these thoughts and patterns emerged and to get to root cause resolution of where these inner critic parts first formed.

I know these parts all too well. I wish I had gotten to know them sooner. I now welcome them and get to know them. I look at the science of the nervous system with awe. My system has been incredible at keeping me safe. I also wish I knew that I was not alone and neither are you. I have found a sisterhood of women just like me. I am so grateful for where this difficult, hurting journey has led me, and I look forward to where I'll be led in the future.

Now I will take you on my journey and how I arrived at where I am at today.

My insecurity and hatred of myself probably started at three years old. I have an excellent memory and I know what I was thinking and feeling as though it were yesterday. Prior to starting Pre-K, I was happy. I had loving parents and grandparents; I was close to my brother. Of course, we fought as siblings do, but we were happy. I had the absolutely most incredible extended family of aunts, uncles and cousins who I saw regularly. My maternal grandparents and a beloved aunt lived with us along with a cousin, Jill who was with us from when she was an infant and I helped with taking care of her from when I was eleven years old. My nurturing parts.

How did this confident little girl with so much love surrounding her become destroyed? I started Pre-K full of joy. I could not wait to attend school with my brother. On the outside, I was this adorable little girl, so well dressed and put together and very girly with gold bracelets adorning my arms. However, I was a tomboy at heart. I loved building forts, jumping in leaf piles and I did always have a little streak of doing exactly what

I pleased. This zest served me well when I finally started to heal.

For example, my mom dressed me perfectly and bought me a perfect backpack. I decided I was taking a dirty bag that I loved with everyone's favorite mouse on it. I won the battle with my mom. That little girl didn't emerge again until her forties.

I attended a private school, and the day before school started a bus came for the public school. My mom said it was a sign and that I should go to public school. My dad and I thought nothing of it. She was right! She is very intuitive.

I was so terribly bullied by most of the girls from Pre-K until 5th grade. If this happened today my teacher most likely would have been fired and the students thrown out of the school.

The girls would accuse me of hitting them, or being mean to them. They would basically project and say I did everything they were doing to me. To this day I loathe hypocrisy. I would often have to miss recess because the teacher would believe them and keep me inside. This was not a punishment to me because recess was torturous for me. Later projection from narcissists would be normal.

The teacher was upset because of my birthday cutoff. My dad pulled strings and had me enter kindergarten and skip Pre-K. I was very intelligent and capable. She was not happy and went as far as sabotaging me, making my parents believe I was dumb and moved me into Pre- K. Even worse, she attempted to have me put into "special classes." Luckily that did not happen. My parents stopped it.

I never spoke a word about my unhappiness until 5th grade because my dad was an educator and told me he would always take the teacher's side. He was and still is kind and doting but because of his experience with his students he felt it was important that I know this. I took it quite literally and learned to keep my mouth shut at an early age. This quiet part will emerge again in my marriage.

The evil witch teacher would ask if I had bags under my eyes or was, I punched? This is where fixating on my flaws occurred and my passive views. I would smell of smoke because my extended family was always over and smoked heavily. This woman would make fun of me almost daily. The teacher would often put me under a piano seat or in the hallway. One time my brother's former teacher saw and asked why I was in the hall. She knew my family well and liked us very much. I said that the teacher hated me. She felt badly. Looking back, I'm sure she was aware of this evil woman but her hands were tied.

Once I was completing *A Little Boy Blue* puzzle with another girl and she said, "so-so can-do puzzles but forget the other one she is so dumb."

Welcome *Hilda*! That first voice of sabotage. Couple the account above with also participating in ballet. I think this is where my body dysmorphia emerged. I was curvy then and the instructors would not allow anyone to wear a tutu. I wanted to cover my butt because I thought my butt and thighs were fat. I also messed up steps and felt that the instructors didn't care for me. I danced to please my parents from three to fourteen. Welcome people pleasing parts.

I had even quit ballet to play baseball at one point and I was thrilled because the boys treated me as a teammate. I was just one of the boys, of course, with my gold bracelets and girlie style. To please my parents, I went back to ballet. I was not happy with this decision, but I sucked it up. My dad was very upset that I quit. I had quit at recital time and the costume I chose came in wrong. Thankfully a sweet girl switched with me. Of course, my mom had to remind me how awful I was to make her switch and quit ballet anyway.

So, we have bullying, ballet and pageants. I was so shy. I now know this was due to the trauma I endured daily at school. My parents thought it was a great idea to put me in pageants at three and four. They did the best they could and always did things out of love, however it was detrimental to a young girl be judged on her looks. I did well, I was 4th runner up in one and won the other. The body dysmorphia was in full effect. I knew every dimple on my body. I would go on to do another pageant in 6th grade and place first runner up, and then in 7th grade I won. It didn't make me feel any better about myself. I never even told my friends I was in one. They read it in the local paper. I will admit that it helped with my shyness and taught me invaluable interview skills. Had I not been so bullied in school it may have not hurt me to be in a pageant.

From first through fifth grade there was still dance and bullying, but my teachers from that point on were wonderful. The bullying from the girls got worse. I have sweaty hands and I now believe this was caused by all of my early childhood trauma. I still sweat. Of the girls no one ever wanted to be my partner, hold my hand, or pick me in sports. I constantly heard, "you're so gross, yuck." The boys were great. I ate alone each day for all those years. It was worse to sit with girls and be humiliated.

Luckily, when I was old enough to read and write and take standardized tests a teacher realized I was incorrectly placed by that original awful teacher. I scored highest in the class on the tests. Without question, she moved me to the top reading group. The damage was done. I was very impatient when I was in the lower groups because I knew I was incorrectly placed. Thank God for that wonderful lady who saw me!

The original class photo from when I was in K and moved to Pre-K surfaced. A bully who was now a year ahead brought it to school to show my entire class that I had been in K and moved down to Pre-K. the demon child literally held it up while my entire class was in line and said, "See, Kim is so dumb she got moved back." Again, I was silent. I would go home and pray for these hurtful children; I would even get choked up and say to myself that they must truly hate themselves to act this way. I can assure you I do not pray for hurtful people anymore. I'm not there yet on my journey.

I held all of this in never fighting back. I was such a people pleaser that when in first grade the kind teacher let us switch seats, I did not move my seat as not to hurt her feelings. In my mind I felt that she chose the first seat for me and I would hurt her if I moved. She was annoyed and told me to move, so I did. I should have told her why I did not move. Later on, I was a better educator because of these experiences. I learned early that you never know what goes on in little one's minds.

I never realized until I was ready to leave my marriage how significantly all of these incidents contributed to me staying in an unhappy marriage. So many protector parts emerged at such a young age. I was people pleasing, staying quiet, making myself small, taking the blame for everything, taking criticism, and experiencing body dysmorphia. I hated myself.

With all I have just accounted I have to add religion. Welcome shame and guilt parts. I am Christian. I was raised Catholic. I still have so much faith, but I'm not as religious. I still say "as" because these Catholic teachings have been so ingrained in me that they're hard to let go. It's also a huge reason why I stayed in my marriage. I viewed it as a sin to leave.

In those early years of school, there were two events that made me feel like I sinned and was going to go to hell. Looking back, I think I had versions of panic attacks. I would lay in bed and tell myself, usually on a Sunday after church, that I was going to die one day and go to hell.

One day, a bully brought cough medicine to school. She gave it to everyone and I took a teaspoon. I know this sounds hilarious now, but at four I convinced myself I was drug addict and a sinner. I'm laughing writing it. What I have learned on my healing journey is the thoughts and perceptions we use to address difficult situations, don't change much as an adult unless we do the work. I also can't believe I took it, because I was a germaphobe even then.

I also prayed for something bad to happen and it did. I believed I was a sinner and I caused it. Someone was supposed to visit, I prayed they didn't come, and they got sick and canceled. Already by this sweet young age I was a sinner condemned to hell, compounded with everything else. I also did not know what an empath was. I was a deep thinker which was not normal for a young child. How did I get here? How was I born to this family in this state?

As I said, the teachers were nice. I was so used to being by myself it didn't matter that no one played with me at recess. The boys did, but I didn't want to bother them. My ability to be alone helped me survive in my marriage. The girls kicked me and kicked dirt at me. One day I finally fought back and pushed a girl. The little hypocrite ran and told on me. The 2nd grade teacher said, "I know Kim and she would never do that unprovoked, so you both are missing recess" I was so happy, could care less about sitting out. I was seen.

To this day lying, unfairness and hypocrisy drive me crazy! Events that transpired after my marriage were the most hypocritical one can imagine and led to me acting out reactively. Reactive abuse is real. It is often used against victims to make them seem unhinged.

I got a little chunky in 5th grade and of course, I was teased at school and at home by my brother and my mom. She really was not mean spirited but it still hurt my feelings. My brother was malicious about it, but I'm sure if he knew it cut me deeply, he would feel terrible. My aunt had cancer and my mom and I was with her for a summer to help her. When my dad came to visit, he didn't recognize me. He never said anything to me, but was upset my mom let this happen. I heard him say that he didn't recognize me and I looked hideous. I was that used to being teased about weight. He would have never been that cruel to my face. He had no idea I heard him. Later in life exes would criticize or value me based on weight and because of previous programming I accepted it. One ex purchased a beautiful coat for me if I dropped weight. I thought nothing of it and dropped the weight.

I was an excellent student, and helpful at home. I cleaned up, was organized, mature and complacent. Even though school was hell and I would cross out kids' faces on school photos my parents did not know I was being humiliated daily. They did not catch on.

My mom would constantly invite the very girls who hurt me over for playdates ignoring my pleas not to. They were sweet in front of her and demons when she wasn't there.

For one birthday Strawberry Shortcake came. I was in 4th grade. I knew I would be tortured the following Monday after the party. My parents were so excited that they planned this and I did not have the heart to tell them I would be made fun of. I kept silent and put my feelings aside. This was also a major theme for me in my marriage.

Another time I knew I was not invited to a sleepover. My mom knew the girl's birthday was approaching and bought her a gift. I was numb when I saw the doll, I did not want to tell her the girl made it clear I was not invited to her party, nor did I want to go. Instead, I said I did not think she was having a party. My mom called the mom and I was now invited. I said nothing and I attended, I was humiliated and reminded at the party that I was not invited and only there because of my mom. Something in me knew I just had to get through childhood.

This theme is familiar later on as well. Of course, my parents and teachers adored me. I would do anything to please them. I sacrificed myself because I did not want to see the hurt look on their faces when they saw I was hurting. I shut up and sucked it up until forty-three. I now know that I was in a freeze fawn response for most of my life.

My parents were loving and caring. I'm not upset with any mistakes they made. I know they worked hard to give us a beautiful life and parented based on their schema. My mom needed perfection from me. I know it came from a loving place and she wanted save me from being made fun of. She was made fun of as a child. Sometimes her actions caused me anxiety and also caused me to be made fun of which was the opposite of what she intended.

She would instruct me to not say or do certain things because if I did those things, I would be made fun of. She was always overly afraid for my safety, so she made me feel as though I had to choose safely. There is a plan. Be your best go to school, be the top, attend college, marry the right person etc. I learned there is no FUCKING plan! I followed the plan and it didn't work. I was angry later after my divorce that I did my part and it blew up! Meanwhile people not following the plan did just great!

Finally in 5th grade my parents started discussing applying me to private middle schools. My current MS only went up to 6th grade. I told my parents about all I had endured from Pre-K. I said there is no way I could attend school with those bitches anymore. I need to get out and go to the public school with the girls I knew from church and my neighborhood. They were so sad and crushed. They felt so badly, that without question they allowed me to attend public school for my last year of lower school. They agreed that I should go in 6th grade to make friends before entering MS in 7th grade.

It was a great decision. I finally listened to myself. I am still best friends with a girl, Katie, that I knew vaguely from church but met that very first day of 6th grade. She was one of my first friends. Even though I should have been distrustful of girls, I had an open heart and I have since been blessed with wonderful friends. These friends got me through my darkest times.

Middle school was fine. *Hilda* was still there with those sabotaging thoughts, "you aren't pretty enough or smart enough, you're fat." My confidence was low. The boys my age were not nice to me. However, I looked like I was 18, and the first day of 7th grade the kids thought I was a teacher. I also was being asked out by really older boys. I would say I can't go out with you because I'm 12. They would apologize and feel silly. It was actually pretty funny. Every time I was mistreated it was my fault, I somehow caused it and deserved it. I loathed myself.

Even though I now had friends, there was always someone to put me down. I liked a boy, and every time he saw me, he would spit at me. Here we go again I thought. Middle school was the only time boys were really mean. Maybe the teasing thing was true that the boys teased girls that they liked. But I felt awful about myself. God, forbid I broke out, there was always a little asshole there to point it out. Another protector part is being overly grateful. Middle school teasing was not as bad as lower school so I took it. I was so grateful that it was detrimental to me because it kept me stuck in situations that I should have broken free from.

I also met my other best friend, Robin we roomed together in college and have never fought. At first, she didn't like me because I dated her friend's ex-boyfriend for a day when we were in 8th grade. She came up to me and yelled at me for dating the boy who was in 10th grade. I don't even know how we became friends. We started talking and hanging out and now I tease her about the first meeting. She has never not been there for me.

By now you are familiar with some of my parts, all which have negatively prepared me how to tolerate behavior I did not like in my marriage and divorce. Let's journey into high school, college and dating. I loved high school 9th grade was my favorite year. There were some normal mean girl things here and there, but all in all it was great. Yet, I still felt inferior, fat, dumb, not good enough. No one who knew me would have thought this.

I was asked out by many seniors. They all thought I was a transfer student because I looked older. You would think I would have so much confidence. Nope. I was top of my class; I had a senior boyfriend. I went to prom in 9th grade. I had many friends, boys and girls. I was class president for 4 years and a majorette. Nothing too awful happened. I loved high school. The inner critic was still there despite all the positive.

However, some boys I dated were controlling. I put up with so much that I should not have. I wish I had learned my lessons then because I would have been saved from future heartache. I didn't do drugs, I was not promiscuous, I didn't drink. Remember premarital sex meant I would burn in hell. I was naïve and still a people pleaser.

I stayed with boyfriends too long when I knew I did not want to. I did not want to hurt them. I put up with them breaking up with me to date others and then come back; I let them control how I dressed. If I went out with girlfriends and they got upset I would have a knot in my stomach and take the blame. These were great habits to benefit whoever my future spouse would be.

During this time, I let my parents have way too much control over me. I was number three in my graduating class. I loved the warmth and wanted to be in Miami. I wanted to be there since I was a child, and I would often say my soulmate is there. Well, now I'm married to someone from south Florida. I applied to my local college and Florida schools. I got almost a full academic scholarship to the University of Miami. The fear-based parenting set in. My dad tried to convince me to stay close. I got scared to leave and I stayed. I still regret it to this day.

My guidance counselor said, "Kim, you can get into pretty much anywhere, apply to top schools." I laughed. A part of me wanted to, but subconsciously I probably did not want to try and fail. Also, my dad, again meaning well, would say you are pretty, you will find a husband, you will be a teacher, you will have the summer off. I did not even want to be a teacher, but I followed "the plan."

I attended a college in my state. I had so many credits from my advanced classes that I graduated a year early and then got my master's degree. Yet still, no one recognized me academically. I was also certified to teach Grades 5-12 and dual certified in social studies and English. My inner voices did not care that I achieved that. I was stupid, not good enough and not worthy. To toxic individuals in my life, I did not make a ton of money therefore, what good were the degrees?

I dated in college and again I let guys shelf me. I was who they wanted to marry after they had fun. I did have a voice though, with outright narcissists. If a guy was a player, I did not bother, I spoke up. It was the subtle, covert kind I had trouble seeing through. I always felt insufficient. I also loved bad boys. I loved them because there were no surprises and they treated me well. Interestingly I did not end up with a bad boy the first time. My current husband is a reformed one and I love it!

My best friend who I lived with had to transfer after our first year of college and I was really sad. I did not become the adult I should have in college because of the school being in close proximity to my parents' home. I was home mostly every weekend. Some of the girls in college were mean and liked that I was younger and could not get in bars and they could. If a guy liked me, they would say things like he likes natural girls, you wear so much makeup, you have big hips and your hair is big. None of which is true but it played into me thinking the guy was too good for me. Hilda the inner critic was always there to protect me. If I thought terrible of myself then no one could hurt me worse then I hurt myself.

I graduated and became a teacher. I did not enjoy this job. I loved the kids and the curriculum but it was not for me. I did it for ten years. As a first-year teacher, I made mistakes and other teachers tried to humiliate me. I was well qualified for one job and the department head was particular and she fought to hire me. I was judged because of how I looked and dressed. One teacher named me in his published book and said I got my job through nepotism. I was unfairly judged often and internalized all of it.

I was a compassionate teacher. I was never going to make someone feel the way I did. I even picked partners for kids so that no one would be left out. I was a better teacher because of my past. I didn't let it dim me.

Throughout my life nothing huge and terrible happened but all of these little cracks and breaks turned me into my worst critic. No one could put me down more than I did. I was an expert. I had no idea why I felt this way but no one ever thought I did. To everyone, I was friendly, popular, smart. To myself I was constantly critical. I have been meaner to myself than anyone on earth. This really gave me what I needed to stay in toxic relationships

I married soon after college. The marriage was a culmination of all the little things that added up to a dysfunctional marriage. To the outside I had the perfect life, inside I was screaming.

Everything I believed about myself was reinforced. I never thought I would leave. I loved him with all my heart and there were many great times. I learned so much from him and have wonderful children. I had two very close people to me die suddenly. One was one of my closest friends' husbands. It awoke me from my coma. I realized life is too short. She has been so supportive of me even in her darkest moments.

As in Lower school I just hung in there until one day I left my marriage. I had to dig deep to find my three-year-old self… the girl before preschool and get that little girl full of vitality back. I was done taking any shit from anyone!

Leaving was so hard. I had all of these ideals in my head, despite these ideals I did it. I'm stronger than ever now. I found my voice. After I left, I fell apart. I went to therapy, I found Caroline Strawson, I took her class. Her methods showed me that all of this baggage didn't need to be there. At forty-six, I learned to love myself. I am lovable, intelligent, kind, and can achieve anything I want. The modalities I use for coaching my clients are the same ones I used for myself. I know they work and that is why it is a passion and mission to help other women.

Hilda is quiet. It is so freeing to love myself and treat myself with love, respect and kindness. I have so much confidence now and I truly believe it and feel it in my body. I use somatic work with my clients where we feel the trauma in our bodies. Trauma is stored in our fascia and cells. I am proud of myself. I never needed to self-soothed with alcohol, drugs or antidepressants. There is nothing wrong with antidepressants I just never needed them.

I have my sad days. I also have complex PTSD, but it is better with all the tools I have to work through it. much of the trauma also caused me to have an autoimmune disease. I feel badly that my children have divorced parents, but I can get myself out of the darkness pretty quickly. I use to cry each time they left to be with the other parent. I use brain spotting on myself and now I don't get as agitated and upset.

You are not stuck. If you are hearing people say move on, get over it, it is not your fault. The brain has not time stamped the trauma. I want to help you! It really is my passion and mission in life. I was that little girl from age three to forty-six who held those silent screams inside herself. Now I'm proud of that little girl for holding it all together. What a miraculous job my nervous system was doing. Now I know the science behind why I felt the way I did.

If I have gotten to where I am today, believe me you can! I am no longer just existing. I'm truly living and experiencing life. I broke free of old ideals and the mentality that kept me caged all of my life. I give zero fucks about what anyone thinks of me. I know how to explore what I'm feeling. This doesn't mean I'm not caring I now have boundaries and I no longer put others feelings ahead of mine. I was raised to make each decision based on everyone else's decisions over mine. Their voices mattered more.

This does not mean that I don't get triggered. Of course, I do, but now I know how to deal with almost anything thrown at me. I am a better wife, mom, daughter, sister and friend now.

If you are reading this know you only need a sliver, a seed of hope to build yourself back. There were days on which I did not care if I woke up. But I had that seed and I grew it into a big ass oak. I can't believe this is my life. I have a career I love; I have a loving husband. We love traveling and being vibrant and I love the relationship I have with my boys.

This entire journey has also broken the cycle of parenting in which I was raised with. I tell my children everything and anything is open to them. Why can't it be you? I also instill in them not to care what others think of you as long as you are being true to yourself and not hurting anyone. Never quiet your voice to stand up for yourself. I also encourage them to use logic and not just emotion when making decisions.

I hope I have touched at least one person with this chapter. If anything, I said has resonated with you please contact me. I would be honored to help you. I wish you a beautiful life!

ABOUT THE AUTHOR
KIM PONTARELLI

Kim Pontarelli is an accredited coach specializing in Narcissistic Abuse Recovery. She has experience with both overt and covert narcissistic healing and uses a trauma informed approach.

Kim is also certified in brain spotting and hypnotherapy. She uses IFS and Positive Psychology in her coaching.

Before coaching and raising her 3 boys, Kim was an educator for 10 years.

She has taught grades one through twelve. Kim has taught Psychology, Law, US History, US Gov't and English at the high school level.

She is dual certified in both Social Studies and English. Kim has experience at the administrative level and holds a Master's degree in education.

Kim mostly enjoys spending time with her husband, three boys and three dogs. She loves to travel and relax as well as trying any new workout.

Kim would love to help coach you to break free from the effects of trauma.

Kim can be reached at:

email: kim@kimpontarellicoaching.com

website: www.kimpontarellicoaching.com

facebook.com/KimberlyPontarelli

instagram.com/kpontarelli1

11

THE SKIN I'M IN

LESLEY LEE

I LOVE MY JOB. I WORK WITH AMAZING PEOPLE FROM ALL OVER the world and I feel that what I do and what I have are enough. I'm very proud that I can feel so positive.

I've managed to put my critical, ruminating thoughts aside, to actually enjoy life. I have allowed calm to seep into my life. But let me tell you, to get here, it's been a long and winding road. I help women understand how they keep making the same mistakes over and over again, inadvertently building a prison for themselves, even though they want something else.

Once we identify what the repetitions are, what drives us to make them, we make a plan to develop a different, far healthier habit. And for those who dare, we go to the root and change the belief that makes us behave the way we do.

Particularly I work with adult children of immigrants and expats who had crappy childhoods. Those that find it difficult to control their anxiety and stress levels. Something they often have in common is a gnawing disquiet. It lies just beneath the surface; a lost sense of belonging, being caught between two or three or more cultures.

You see, that was me before I worked on myself. I was the type of person who just couldn't 'switch off', let go, enjoy life, enjoy the moment, enjoy my family. A little too quick-tempered. Being anxious and highly-strung had become a habit, an addiction. It was my high, like tequila or cocaine. Like a junkie, I needed my fix of adrenaline. I was constantly working late and didn't have much time to be with my husband, children, let alone friends.

In work there had been a lot on my plate. But even so, I wondered how my colleagues seemed able to handle the stresses so easily. I felt that I took longer, and even when the work was finished, it just didn't seem quite right, something was missing, it could've been better. Even when the task seemed straight forward, I managed to make it complicated. Crippling perfectionism turned into chronic procrastination. Working so many late nights became a habit, and then the brain fog set in, the lack of focus, indecisiveness. I was always exhausted and tended to eat too much of the wrong things to try and boost my energy.

Far too often I found myself zoning out and turning to Youtube or Facebook, too tired to do anything else. And whenever I had to make a presentation, something would always happen. If I was lucky it was a headache but more usually it was a migraine or a cold or a fever. It's almost as if I was unconsciously sabotaging my best efforts. Soon enough I just fell out of love with my work, lost all motivation.

Thinking back, it wasn't the first job where this had happened either, I noticed that I had felt like this in my previous job and the one before that. When I decided to make a career change and start training as a Coach, I soon realized that it was not the work, it was ME. It was my own mindset and how I viewed the world that drove me to be so anxious. But what exactly made me think that way?

Being in the pandemic lockdown felt eerily familiar to me in more ways than one. I suppose I first became aware of it when I saw a YouTube video about a group of Chinese children who were growing up in the UK. They said that they couldn't quite understand why people on the streets would call them 'the coronavirus' and tell them to go back home. As soon as I heard that I involuntarily stopped breathing and then was left gasping, tears rolling down my face. It's as if I'd blocked my own sad memories behind a wall and just like in the story, the dam broke, and all those memories flooded back.

Whilst growing up in the 70s, in a large northern city in England, the same thing was still going on, except the excuse and the names had changed. 'Chinese, Japanese – don't forget to wash your knees.' It was kind of a non-sensical song and if you sang it to a Chinese person who had never heard it before they would probably not even realize what it was about. But being taunted by it on a regular, at times daily basis, I knew exactly what it was about. I suppose by the time I was in primary school, I started to realize that people saw me as different, as the other, not one of them. That I was wrong, that I didn't fit in, that I didn't belong. As I grew, I learned to dodge gangs of boys and sometimes girls, to cross the road or walk back the way I had come and go the long way round to get home or wait around the corner until the danger had passed. It hurt to see those who I thought of as friends, part of the groups who called me names. The sharp sting of betrayal was something that I never quite got used to.

Decades later, on a therapist's couch when those memories were safely tucked up in a box, suddenly the song came back to my mind, an earthy, agar-like smell came to my nostrils. The agar smell I would recognize years later as I grew bacterial cultures in a biology lab. In my mind's eye, I could imagine a small unknowing child smelling her knees, befuddled, and wondering why everyone kept on telling her to wash them.

Even in the candy stores, I always seemed to find myself at the back of the queue - or was it my imagination. Mmm, the candy store, my favorite place. I loved buying the chocolate Penguin bars, the ones in the green wrapper were my favorite. I swear they were mint-flavored, even though the shopkeeper insisted they were all the same, whatever color the wrapper. I loved them and the chocolate covered marshmallow biscuit Wagon Wheels, with the inevitable picture of a cowboy in the Wild West.

As I got older, the singing stopped but the messages got stronger and more to the point. F@*! of home ch***! (this last word rhymes with pink). It didn't help that I lived near to my secondary school and hundreds of children would pass by my home sniggering and getting in as many insults in as they could.

It was like a sporting event. Interestingly, it was more of a group sport, very rarely did a lone kid try to call me names, it was always in the presence of others. I suppose it was all bravado, a way of ranking higher with the other males. It still hurt all the same. As an adult, it became the other way around, it was a lone sport, furtively whispered under breath when nobody else was around.

It wasn't everyone, there were some really lovely kids who didn't think it was right and tried to defend me or ignore the meanspirited ones, cautious not to get involved, for fear of becoming victims themselves. Voicing equality directly to bullies was not for the fainthearted. But the name-calling happened often enough that I did indeed feel that I was an ugly thing, not to be touched or associated with. When playing Catch the girls, kiss the girls, I was doomed never to be caught, despite not being that quick on my feet.

Why be so mean? If it wasn't for these eyes, this wide nose and thick lips, I would be deemed normal. I would fit in. I would not be noticed. I would slip under the radar. For so many years it was my greatest wish to be normal, to fit in, to not have to be careful about what I say, to try not to be too bold, to not be scared for getting above my station, for fear of being put down, of being put in my place. But alas, my eyes never became rounder, my nose never became thinner or grew a bridge. I was doomed to stand out in a crowd forever. Regrettably, I became ashamed of the skin I'm in.

To stay safe and out of the line of attack, I tried to blend in with the background, keep quiet, be nice, be a good girl. Not be opinionated, not pose a threat, not ask any awkward questions and then, for the most part, my presence would be tolerated. Friends would say proudly, 'no, she's not one of them, she's one of us.' And I used to feel grateful for this consideration, this tolerated acceptance. But even at this young age, I had a twinge that something wasn't quite right. It was meant as a compliment but actually…it was not and my young mind couldn't quite work out, why not. So as long as I behaved in the way that I thought others wanted me to behave, I became all that my whole life I wanted to be…normal!

No longer shunned but accepted by the people who knew me, and we all kept up the pretence quite well. We all pretended. It was our open secret. And I was able to fool myself, until I saw my reflection in the mirror and then remembered that I, for some, was an unwelcome guest, who could be insulted and humiliated at their whim because I didn't count. My feelings didn't count. I didn't matter to them. I was definitely under the impression that I could not complain, I had no right to dignity.

As an immigrant, there are some things that you have to hang up and say goodbye to at the front door. Now whereas I was too Chinese outside my front door, on the other side I was just not Chinese enough. It was only the thickness of a piece of wood, but it could just as well have been a continent. By passing over the threshold, I travelled through space and time to where I lived a parallel life, the obedient Chinese daughter "me". Without even noticing it, I became a chameleon taking on the colors and textures of my surroundings. It allowed me to blend in, to not stand out but there was a price to this invisible skill. It was as if my wholeness was divided up. I was merely a sum of parts that had to please others. And in the place of wholeness, there was only emptiness. My life was not mine to live. It seemed that this was not allowed. It belonged to others and the identities that they wanted me to have. Thought I should have. Or at least that was what the little "me" learned.

On the Chinese side of the door my dad did his best to look after me. Bring me up well. But his expectations were sky-high.

My memories at the beginning of primary school, are what I would call normal, kind of rosy. But as the years passed and I got older, a darkness crept into those feelings. Memories are few and far between. There is however, one memory that stays with me. It was when, for the first time, I became consciously aware of the gorilla that dwelled amongst us. I'm not sure what I noticed first. Was it the baring of the teeth, the curling of his now red lips or the wild eyes? I'm sure my memory must be exaggerated. It was probably an innocuous situation. But through my child's imagination, working overtime, I swear his hair stood up on his head and he looked like King Kong. Just like Peter Banner turned into the Hulk, he literally turned into a gorilla before my eyes. I had proudly told him that I came 2nd in the maths test and he growled that I should have come 1st. That I'll never be any good. I winced at his comments. Always wanting to please but never quite pulling it off. I didn't realize this was his way of motivating me, guiding me to do better. At that young age, I did not realize I was listening to the words of an over-tired, struggling father.

The message that I did understand is that "You are not good enough. You will never be good enough. You are flawed." My subconscious made a note to self. 'Pride goes before a fall. Don't get too full of yourself. Stay safe and play small.' Defeated, I slunk away, disappointed in myself and wondering how I always seemed to miss the mark. I cried for the warm embrace of a mother that I knew would never be coming. Who would comfort me and tell me that everything would be okay? No-one. There was nobody there for me. And thus, food became my trusty companion, that distracted me from the pain of not being good enough.

When the tears stopped, I could see a Wagon Wheel cookie under the bed. But even before reaching out to eat it, it had already turned to ash in my mouth. Is this the moment that lost faith in myself? It's amazing how such seemingly insignificant moments can give birth to long-lasting limiting beliefs. "I can never do anything right. I will always disappoint others."

Ever since that moment or maybe it was before, I feel like a quiet almost inaudible voice has been reminding me, 'Don't. Don't. Don't do it.' Whether it was in front of my father, whether at work, with friends or with any type of authority figure. The voice sends the urgent message, 'Don't. Don't think you are anything special. Don't be seen. Stay invisible. Do your best to please and you'll escape the criticism.' But what hurt more than the words was the feeling of being a burden, that I was a cross to bear. I was not good enough and it was my fault and I was resented for it.

Every time I heard his key turning in the front door, I froze to the spot. Who would be walking through the door? Would it be my dad? Or the critical gorilla? The best I could hope for was to be ignored. I tried to become the invisible man and disappear into the armchair, become the armchair. Not make a sound. Tried not to breath too loudly. I would hide my crossed fingers behind my back, 'Please God, don't let him see me.' He pretended not to.

In the end, we came to the unspoken agreement to ignore each other. We lived in a house of ghosts that couldn't see each other...except, we could. It was a strange arrangement, but it seemed it was the best, most peaceful option available to us. Was this around the time that I learned to become afraid being in the skin I'm in?

Finally, in my twenties I left home, I felt that I had escaped the oppressive, disapproving eye of criticism. I travelled the world, having adventures. I was FREE! Except, I wasn't. Little did I know that the oppressive, disapproving eye not only came with me but that I had become its new owner. I became the critic.

Looking back at my childhood, I can see that I was in a constant state of running away, hiding and feigning invisibility. Unfortunately, I became used to and almost addicted to the adrenaline high of being in flight, running away, and difficult to settle.

Highly-strung some said. I became a runner and the avoider. But it was impossible to sustain this high and inevitably I would crash and be in bed for days. My safe place. And when invisibility was not available, likeability, niceness, agreeableness became my shields against imagined attack or rejection. A way to stay safe. I became the people-pleaser. Equally as exhausting.

As a youngster I had made sleep my beloved sanctuary, there I didn't disappoint, I didn't have to please, I didn't have to hide or be small. When I laid down it felt like warm treacle enveloping me, I just felt that sinking feeling, falling into a comfortable slumber, falling to the bottom of a warm pool where I was safe enough to be me. Normal. No need for struggling, faking or awkwardness.

I became a sleeper. And when I couldn't sleep, I ate. I became an over-eater. I've slept so many years away that I thought that I must have a deadly disease. A disease that had not been discovered yet. After many years of searching, I've finally found the cause for this disease. Abandon, shame and the resulting anxiety. It's a disease of the mind, of faulty beliefs about yourself and the world, that were created from lived experiences from an early age and the resulting interpretations of a child's mind, trying to make sense of the world. I became a constant worrier. Confused. "Why did others reject me so much?".

In contrast, when I couldn't hide and needed to get things done, I was able to use worry, anxiety and eventually panic to click into overdrive. Running on high energy became a lifestyle for me and I needed to create strategies to feed the habit.

Leaving things to the last minute, packing only hours before a flight. Procrastination was the perfect way to maintain that adrenaline high. That was my life, running full speed ahead or exhausted and motionless. The middle ground did not exist. It seemed to work fine, that is, until the menopause hit. And then, it was time to pay the piper. There was no more bounce in the ball, the elastic had broken. My energy levels fluctuated and became unpredictable. I could no longer pull the rabbit out of the hat and wow the audiences as I used to. I could no longer pull all-nighters and work at the rate I used to.

How to deal with this?

I started to get panic attacks, miss deadlines, and lose total confidence in myself. Spending more and more time working, I had less time to spend time with my kids. We all suffered. And the gorilla that mainly remained dormant for years, raised its ugly head and roared. I could no longer maintain the haphazard existence that I was used to. My anxiety attacks pushed me to change my life.

The long road to eventually become that person and have the life I always wanted started way back when I became a Life Coach ten years ago. I learned to shift my mindset. What a revelation! There are different ways to see the world, not only through my pessimistic, hypervigilant lens. I found effective tools to set goals, develop strategies, plan. But still the anxiety persisted. I knew that still something was wrong, but it lay beyond my reach. Like an itch in the middle of my back. I knew the itch was there, I just couldn't reach it. So I kept looking for the right way to get to it. I kept searching.

Reading an article, I recognized many of the symptoms that showed up in my life. And it was a relief, a relief to know finally what I was dealing with. This is what really accelerated my journey along the path of healing. I was suffering the effects of developmental trauma. Trauma that is experienced as you develop as a child. At first sight, this word seemed so exaggerated, so dramatic. What actually is trauma? Here are a couple of definitions that have brought me clarity:

> "A single or multiple or enduring experiences, that overwhelm the person's ability to cope or integrate the experience (senses, ideas, emotion, predicative) as a whole. It is unexpected, unpredictable, the person is not prepared, and it goes beyond their control. It has long lasting effects because it has not been resolved."
>
> — WEINER, I. B., & CRAIGHEAD, W. E.

> "A threat to life (or one's well-being, one's survival), when one is in a state of helplessness."
>
> — R. SCAER

It's almost as if growing up in an environment of fear has led me to focus on thoughts of survival rather than those of joy. In just the past twenty years so many amazing advances have been made in understanding the mind and brain and how they are so intimately linked to the body, emotions, and indeed, our very soul. In order to scratch that itch, I dived in and tried them all.

I learned that it is not only possible to manage symptoms and develop action plans to get your life on track but often a deeper work accessing the subconscious can change limiting beliefs. Those beliefs that invisibly hold you back and keep you small. It's as if they're wrapped up, hidden out of sight and we don't even realize they are there. But they pop-up on a daily basis, revealing themselves as beliefs or thoughts, 'I am less than. Others are better than me. There is something wrong with me. I am always wrong. I'm not… (good, clever, beautiful, handsome, worthy, normal) enough'. All those beliefs that we never tell anyone but keep as a secret. Many times, going to extreme lengths so nobody would ever find out. Now I could understand where my perfectionism came from. It was an effort to hide that I was not good enough. Why I felt I couldn't say No, for fear of being rejected and left alone.

Understanding was indeed a revelation, but it was not enough. I had to unlearn this way of thinking, this habit of a lifetime and replace it with a better way of thinking. Which instead of keeping me stuck, within safe limits, of my comfort zone, pushed me beyond them into new unknown territories. It was when I learned about parts theory that the penny finally dropped.

I realized the purpose of being the good girl, the chameleon, the critic, the avoider, the outsider, the invisible man, the sleeper, the over-eater, the worrier, the perfectionist, the procrastinator and the gorilla. Through Internal Family Systems, I learned that they were all part of the family that resided within me. Loving me and protecting me the best way they knew how. At times they became clumsy, uncoordinated or they'd get in the way of each other.

So what did this look like? Imagine if I arrived at a new social club and wanted to make friends. The good girl part would take the driver's seat and try to fit in and turn into the people-pleaser.

The people-pleaser would predictably try to do too much, accommodate too much, self-sacrifice too much. That's when the rebel would grow tiresome, kick her out and inevitably get me into trouble. She was no doormat and suffered no fools. In an effort to put limits and keep me safe, she had no qualms about being rude or just plain antagonistic. And on occasion, even more drastic, the gorilla got involved if I felt particularly threatened. The avoider would inevitably help me to run away and either the over-eater or the sleeper would show up to distract me and fill my face or make me forget my problems for a couple of hours. Dissociation is an amazing survival tool. The ultimate protection against the hurt.

To interrupt these repetitive behaviors, I have learnt that introducing new members to my internal family have helped me feel grounded when I want to flee, put boundaries when I want to over please, to dialog, explain and negotiate when I want to scream and destroy. I have learned to nurture, hug and love the gorilla, so he doesn't feel alone, helpless and threatened. And slowly, he allowed me to see that he was actually a she - the little girl that felt so rejected, hiding in a gorilla suit disguise.

Feeling that she needs to be scary in order not to be hurt. It reminds me of the scene in the Wizard of Oz, when the wizard comes out from behind his hiding place and allows himself to be seen. Just a normal person building up a false persona, to make up for his perceived inadequacies.

I intentionally, build a home for her so she feels that she is loved, that she is worthy, that she is enough just as she is. She does not need to change anything. Obviously, this is a much-simplified version of what really goes on but I think you get the gist. On my own personal path, I have sung, I have danced, painted, journaled, breathed, shouted, cried, mourned, loved and cared my way back to balance and health.

I have learned that the discrimination that I faced as a child was not because there was anything wrong with me. It was because the bullies did not know how to deal with their own pain and merely passed it on. Misery loves company. I have come to understand my parents and see them just as they are. Normal people just like you or I. In deep meditations, I have seen two little children maybe four or five years old, running, laughing and playing in long grass. Looking into each other's eyes, trusting, loving, cherishing each other's company. I am one child, and my father is the other. It makes me think that we are both beautiful beings, living this earthly existence, the best way we can. The only difference is, we grew up in different moments of time.

He was never one to talk of the past. I don't know much about his, but I do know a little. At times I wonder what it was like for him to grow up as a teenager in Japanese-occupied China, to escape the cruelty and hunger onto a merchant ship. How did the other sailors treat this youngster? How did he manage in that tough, masculine world without the softness of his mother, without the company of his family? Not even knowing if they were alive. What traumas was he forced to live so that he could survive?

Even though he died many years ago, I still connect with the memory of him now, after so many decades of disliking him, being so afraid of him, in my healing, I can see him through different eyes. I understand that compared to the life that he lived he was doing good by me. He provided me with a house and food that he didn't have when he was younger. That was how he showed me his love. My life was infinitely easier than his.

There were no hugs and kisses, no kind words. Emotions were a luxury, but it was a safety that he did not experience. Despite working on a ship for many years, literally being on water every single day, he never learned how to swim. I wonder how scary that would have been for him. How much fear the constant threat of falling overboard generated in his body? Or even worse, being threatened with being thrown overboard if he didn't do what others wanted. In one somatic therapy session, an image of a young teenager, came to my mind, breathlessly crawling up the shore out a stormy sea. The fear that I felt in my own body was palpable.

Was this my imagination? A metaphor? Or was it a memory passed down through my father's genes? Intergenerational trauma is a thing, you know. Whatever the interpretation, through my own personal work, I find peace in being able to relate to my father and the memory of him through a different lens. Once processed, I can start to let go of the denser, more emotionally charged memories and the lighter ones start to shine through.

The ones where he was kind, he did try to make an effort. Where he did try to play hide and seek with me. It must have been difficult being a single parent trying to bring up a little four-year-old girl, all on his own.

Even though my journey has been painful, I am grateful for all that it has taught me. The knowledge and understanding it has gifted to me. I can now sit in my fear, anger, envy, shame, anxiety and whatever other emotions pop up. I am able to hold them and allow them to wash through me, even though it is uncomfortable, and my instinct is to repress them. I permit them to protect me by delivering their message. Yes, this is what I believe emotions are for. They are our body's way of communicating with us. I sit still and listen and take heed of their wisdom 'be careful, be brave, stand up for yourself, stop being complacent, connect to others, let go and move on' and many other things too numerous to mention.

I have done the inner work and let my parts know that I have grown up, that I am now the adult in the room and that I will take charge.

Do what I need to do, to not feel so helpless ever again. I learned to be the parent for myself, the one that I had always wished to have. I vow to break the cycle of trauma that previously was handed down from one generation to another.

It stops with me.

I can proudly say that I am accepting and loving the skin I'm in. I feel so lucky to be able to accompany others when their path through life becomes difficult. I help them make sense of the pain, together we unpack the half-remembered stories, feel for the memories that stay just out of reach. Together we consciously work on how they want their lives to be and develop a plan to make it happen. They learn how to let go of the pain that got stuck in their bodies. And they learn a methodology to do that with or without me by their side. The aim is for them to become incredibly resilient and confident, knowing that whatever situation arises in their lives, they have the knowledge, resources and coping skills to deal with it. Armed with this confidence my clients have managed to leave unhealthy relationships when previously, they felt trapped and unable to survive on their own. They have graduated with master's degrees and PhDs even though lack of self-confidence and imposter syndrome had them put off finishing their thesis for many years. Not to mention all of the women who have overcome shame and anxiety and with confidence, have stepped into the limelight of their own lives, allowing themselves to be seen for who they truly are. I marvel at their results.

Given my own history, I find it particularly fulfilling to work with the adult children of immigrants. How is an immigrant different from the child of an immigrant? In my mind, an immigrant, as a child, has been immersed in the same culture as their parents, grandparents, extended family, neighbors, and community. They share a common language, a similar set of values or way of seeing the world. They have shared the same stories, songs and traditions as they grow up TOGETHER.

For me, as I have experienced it, for I am the child of an immigrant, there was a disconnect, a lack of community to which I felt I belonged. This is probably not an academic definition, but this is how I have lived this experience, trying to find the words as best I can, to describe what happened to me, to make sense of the repercussions and how it has hindered and enriched life.

I have the immense good fortune to be able to work with clients, in a space where the latest scientific discoveries meet ancient wisdom. Accompanying women go from overworked, self-critical & distracted to free, self-appreciative & present in less time is such a satisfying experience. I am so passionate about sharing holistic approaches, that give them the relief from stress & anxiety they need to live their best lives. I have been told by those that I've worked with that I have a knack for finding clarity in the confusion and listening beyond the words they say, helping them heal and manifest an ideal lifestyle on their own terms. By expressing our authentic selves and connecting with our true power, I am confident that it IS possible to lead an ultimately peaceful life for years to come – without falling back into old self-sabotaging habits.

To all of you who may be passing through difficult moments in your lives, I would like to encourage you to never give up, no matter how hopeless you feel, there is always hope. Things on the outside don't necessarily have to change, it is the change on the inside that really matters. I have a feeling that my story could be similar to that of any child who has suffered discrimination, those that were considered different by the people around them.

Whether it be the way they look, think or behave. If that is you, my heart goes out to you.

I see you, I hear you, I understand your pain.

You are worthy.

You are enough.

You have the right to take up and occupy the space you are in.

I encourage you to start to do the inner work, just take the first step and the path will open up. As well as the mind, work on the body, which is where the pain is stored. And just as importantly, find your tribe, those that are positive and accept you. They are out there somewhere, it's just a matter of connecting.

ABOUT THE AUTHOR
LESLEY LEE

Lesley Lee MSc. is a multicultural, trauma-informed Life Coach.

She helps adult children of immigrants and expats who had crappy childhoods recover their balance, health and self-confidence. Growing up as the daughter of Chinese immigrants in a large northern city in the UK was her first experience of living between cultures. In her early 30s, she moved to South America and has lived there for the last 20 years.

She has two beautiful and amazing teenage children, a marvellously supportive husband and three curious cats.

Looking back on this unique experience, she reflects on the experience of being different and all that it entails. And in quieter moments you can find her pondering the deeper meaning of topics such as belonging, home and acceptance.

After certifying as a Professional Ontological Coach in 2010, she has also certified as a Life Coach, Cultural Orientations Framework Coach, Narcissistic Trauma Informed Coach, Breath Coach and Rapid Transformational Therapy Practitioner amongst other modalities.

She has also served as a Director of the International Coach Federation ICF, Peru Chapter and lectured at the Pontifical Catholic University of Peru.

You can reach Lesley at www.theunfoldinglotus.com

12

THE REJECTION WOUND : HOW TO HEAL AND SET YOURSELF FREE

NOSHIELA MAQSOOD

As I sit here writing, I'm filled with a mixture of emotions. Looking back at my life, even five years back, if someone had told me I would be where I am today, helping women to heal from their trauma, empowering them to become generational change makers... I would have laughed and never believed them.

If someone told me I would have appeared on television numerous times to share my story and my works, I never would have believed them.

If I had been told I would be nominated for awards, become a best-selling author and train women all over the world, to help other women to heal, grow and evolve... I would never have believed them.

That's the thing that holds so many of us back. Not believing in ourselves. We limit ourselves based on our current situation and our past. We carry so much emotional baggage and refuse to let go until it becomes too much to bear. So many women hold themselves back because they unconsciously prioritise what other people think of them. That was me and this might be you right now too.

My name is Noshiela Maqsood and I am the founder of The Empowered Muslimah Academy® and the Director of Noshiela Noor Coaching and Training Ltd. I have the honour of empowering women to heal from their past so they can create generational change. I coach women on a one-to-one basis, I run a healing programme and I train women to master their mindset and emotions. I am a trainer of Neuro Linguistic programming, Timeline therapy® and Hypnotherapy. By learning from me, women are obtaining knowledge and skills that are out of the ordinary. They learn how to change their thinking, how to identify patterns in their behaviours, address their emotions and hidden wounds so they live a life of contentment, passion and purpose.

I coach women who:

- Have been abused.
- Neglected.
- Have been through domestic violence.
- Lack confidence and self-esteem.
- Struggling with anxiety, depression, grief, betrayal and hurt.

Every woman that I've worked with has showed up with her wounds, her own story, tears and pain. After doing the inner work and healing the unseen wounds, the same women step into their power, embrace their strengths and their beautiful scars.

The more women I coached, the similar themes I noticed and really began focusing on coaching Muslim women, that's when I created The Empowered Muslimah Academy®. I support women from all faiths and backgrounds, I just realised where I needed to laser focus.

I think women are amazing, strong, powerful, precious, caring and loving beings. We have unique God given gifts and talents that allow us to touch the lives of others, whether that be our family members, friends, colleagues or communities. Often as women we lose ourselves in the pursuit of pleasing others and catering to the needs of others, that we make ourselves the last priority.

What's scary and true for many women is not knowing the difference between being kind and being a people pleaser. You may have heard this time before or you may be wondering what a people pleaser is exactly. A people pleaser is someone who is overly concerned with other people's opinion of them.

From a very young age, I remember, all I wanted to feel like I belong somewhere. I wanted people to appreciate me and praise me when I did something good. When you're one of seven siblings, its wasn't the top priority for our parents to make sure we were emotionally doing well. They did the best that they could with the knowledge, understanding and resources they had.

My mother came to this country from Pakistan at the Young age of nineteen, she married my father and dedicated her life to serving her in laws, my father and then her children. Although my mum was seen as a super woman, she wasn't emotionally empowered which resulted in me as a child constantly searching for that emotional connection that I found in my father. Regardless of your background, family structure or anything else, a child will always want to be told they're loved, they want to feel loved, and they will give meaning to love based on what they see as children.

As a child, I remember being on edge and wondering if my mum was in a good mood or a bad mood so I could plan what to say or not to say. I was constantly finding ways of proving I was good enough and also felt responsible for the emotional well being as a child. It was tiring and confusing.

I had painted a picture in my head of the perfect Muslim girl.

She was quiet because being loud was immodest. She was dutiful and did as her elders said otherwise she was disrespectful and a disgrace even. The perfect Muslim girl was obedient and never questioned orders given to her. She was supposed to sacrifice her aspirations and wishes to suit others because a huge part of being a Pakistani Muslim girl was ruled by 'WHAT WILL PEOPLE SAY?'

The amount of lives ruined because of this statement is unbelievable. It just shows why I became such a people pleaser!

My father was quite laid back whilst my mother was very strict. I often felt like I didn't have a voice of my own. I wasn't allowed to have opinions. Who was I to want to be successful?

I was the kid that wanted to be rich and famous, so I was figuring it out in my head, 'girl, how is this going to work out?"

Slowly, I began giving up on my desire for education, the desire to learn new things. I just felt like life was pointless.

People pleasing, not feeling good enough, lack of self-esteem mostly route back to our early years.

Its only in my late twenties, when I began my healing journey, I realised I was a complete people pleaser. I had no boundaries and was thinking I was being kind yet in fact I was going out of my way to make sure people were happy with me even if I wasn't.

I struggled to say No to others even for the smallest things and I believe that this lead to a lot of people taking advantage of me because they knew I was always going to say Yes.

I remember I was the friend who constantly said Yes. I was the sibling that always said Yes. I was the child that always said Yes because all I wanted was approval and acknowledgment. I just wanted to be told how good I was or how hard I tried. When that didn't happen, I internalised the lack of response as 'I need to do more', 'I'm not good enough', 'I need to work harder'.

These beliefs have caused a lot of trouble in my life. Trust me, I've done some absurd things to prove I was good enough! Don't we all at some point in our lives?

As time went on, I found myself being very connected to my father. He came to England at the age of six and has spent most of his life here, so his values and mindset wasn't so fixed although traditional and cultural values were equally as important to him. Me and my father used to spend a lot of time together, I used to ask him questions around religion that I was often confused about. By learning from my dad and my own self initiated learning, I finally understand the difference between culture and religion. I truly believe at a certain point in my life, I had an identity crisis until I gained clarity.

I learned so many beautiful things about my faith that gave me comfort and solace. I learnt I could be unapologetically me without having to meet anyone's criteria of what I should be like.

I learnt, God wants me to be happy and loves me. Before that I was always afraid of God and being punished.

Al - Wadud is one of the names of God which means the most loving.

The more I continued to learn, the easier it was for me to differentiate between culture and religion and I began falling in love with my faith.

There are so many amazing Muslim women in history that impacted to society in a positive way.

In order to overcome this identity crisis, I was learning about significant Muslim figures that I could look up to. Following the teachings of prophet Muhammad, peace be upon Him, I finally saw the truth about women.

Before His prophet Hood, the Arabs used to bury baby girls alive and had no respect for women. He changed the narrative and taught people how to be kind, loving, compassionate and merciful to ALL. Not just men and not just women. Not just Muslims but mankind as a whole.

As my journey of connecting deeper with my faith continued, I became even closer to my father as we would pray together, learn religion together and recite the Quran together.

At the age of nineteen, my parents parted ways. My dad left and didn't come back. For eight years I hardly saw my dad and it was the hardest thing to face and accept.

I was still a part of a family of eight other people but I felt so alone. I would wait and hope he would return. I slowly started losing my sense of identity. How could it be?

I felt like an abandoned five-year-old. Lost. Helpless. Heartbroken. Confused. The days went on and he never returned. I felt like I was grieving the loss of my best friend, my guide, my father. I'd never felt a pain like it before. I blamed myself.

To help cope, I started working three jobs! Three different jobs in one day. Nothing filled the void but it helped me to cope.

A couple of years later, I married my now husband. This in itself was like a world war as I wasn't allowed.

In the end the marriage took place and the truth is, I was in for a surprise. Being a people pleaser, losing myself after my parents split and wanting somewhere I could call home wasn't a good combination. I wasn't to know at the time. I didn't have the self-awareness or knowledge.

Getting married, falling pregnant straight away, dealing with in-laws and their commands. It wasn't the best start. You see now I can see that I came into the marriage with unhealed trauma, a load of emotional baggage expecting the best from it and expecting my husband to be superman and fix it all!

Unfortunately, it was the opposite. There were a lot of clashes, misunderstandings and unfair treatment in the beginning so me and my husband decided to live separately which is something we had already discussed and agreed. I gave birth to my first child and a few months later, I found myself caught up in a never-ending web of lies and corruption. The people pleaser part of me came into full play here!

Before I knew it, I was involved in a court case for fraudulent votes and perverting the course of justice. I did not vote and never had to be honest, yet I was emotionally blackmailed to say I did as someone else has impersonated to be me, who then got caught. I had just given birth to my baby girl, I was struggling with my emotions after giving birth and had all of this piled onto me. Because the people involved were close to my husband, it was hard for me to tell the truth because I knew the consequences it would have on them. In reality, I shouldn't have cared and should have saved my own back but the people pleasing part of me took over, I thought I was saving someone.

My lack of self esteem and self-worth as well as the emotional blackmail pushed me to continue.

Whilst the trial was ongoing, I fell pregnant with my second child which made it even harder. I truly believe she was given to me as a gift, as a lesson, as a beautiful soul who became my light at the end of the dark tunnel. I struggled to sleep as I would have nightmares of being in prison and giving birth to my baby inside. I stopped going out as I felt humiliated as it was shared on television and in the newspapers. (This isn't the kind of fame I wanted as a child.)

In the end it was a huge case that went to trial, and I was so close to being sentenced to prison. Instead, I ended up with 250 community hours. I was relieved to be able to come home to my daughter and try to relax for the rest of my pregnancy. It ended in July, and I gave birth to my baby girl in September. It didn't stop there, because although I escaped a physical prison cell, I hadn't escaped the mental cage. Over time my mental health went down hill. I began isolating myself. My relationship with my husband went down hill. I faced a lot of hurt, betrayal, grief within my initial years of marriage. Before I knew it, I had lost control of my emotions and began self harming. I felt alone. The only support I had, was my family who always did their best to be there for me.

One evening, I sat in my room in the dark, I called out to God and said 'Oh Allah, please show me a sign, help me through this, show me some light...'

Within the hour, I received a message on my phone from one of my friends that read 'Allah only changes the situation of a believer, if they change themselves.'

That's when the penny dropped. I had been in victim mode for so long and realised I needed to do something about it.

I was scrolling on Facebook that night and came across a coach, a life/business coach. I thought what the heck is one of those? I snooped around her profile and realised this lady could potentially help me get myself back together! I messaged her and bombarded her with my craziness and told her I needed help to move on. We arranged a call and took it from there. I hired my first coach and its THE best thing I ever ever did. She helped me to understand myself better, she helped me heal my unseen wounds, she helped me step into power and find my passion which led to me training to become a certified coach and I began to coach women. I, me, the Muslim Pakistani girl who had to quieten down, I started coaching women and helping them to heal!

I then trained as a trainer and I now coach and train women so they can help themselves and others. I'm dedicated to creating a legacy of healed women. Cycle breakers. Change makers!

I want you to know, regardless of your faith, background, and what your story is... you can get through this.

I truly believe that God only burdens a soul with what they can bear. You are powerful enough to overcome it all and find your true self once again.

When the Prophet Muhammad ruled, women were given rights, they were supported and respected as they should be.

I realised how much of my limitations, fears and frustration were from my upbringing. Slowly things started to make sense and I began to differentiate between religion, culture and my own personality.

The running theme of all my life's occurrences was REJECTION. I had to heal my rejection wound in order to flourish. The rejection wound was created from my childhood and later life traumatic experiences.

Its amazing isn't it, how most of what's happening right now in your life will be back tracked to your childhood? Without you even realising, you can connect the dots from your current situation and your childhood. A lot of people I work with often say, 'I had a good childhood...' When people say this, I question, good based on what? And whose standard? Children accept their circumstances because its something they're not in control of.

From the language that's used to the emotions parents are feeling, impact the child's life on a deeper level than one realises.

I speak to some amazing Muslim women, who have great passions and ideas, yet for some reason deep within, they stop themselves.

I myself have experienced what it feels like to so badly want to make a change, to create the life I wanted, yet there was something within that kept stopping me.

Was it my intuition? NO! What I'm referring to here is the inner critic. The inner critic is the constant chatter formed from the rejection wound.

Healing the rejection wound.

When beliefs of males being more privileged heavily influenced your upbringing, you naturally fear rejection because your mind has stored the idea of you not being important and valid.

If you're used to hearing things like:

You're never going to be successful.

What do you know?

Who going to listen to you?

And even more subtle statements like:

- I haven't got time for this.
- You're too loud.
- Stop showing off.
- No one wants to know.

If you were rejected when you needed connection from your parents, peers and other adults, your brain and body store this as not being wanted, seen or heard because the feeling that comes with being rejected is too painful, you're constantly going to want to hide away, play small and avoid showing off your talents.

The rejection wound can show up in many forms with the recurring theme of being afraid of being judged, criticised, and abandoned, which all come under the rejection wound.

As a result of not acknowledging and healing your rejection wound, it manifests in all areas of your life and is displayed through your thoughts and behaviours that come from a place of fear rather than conviction and certainty.

Limiting beliefs about yourself are formed from emotionally significant events in your life. If the rejection is something you struggle with a lot, it will impact how you feel about yourself.

Do you often feel like:

- You're not good enough.
- You're not smart enough.
- You're not pretty enough.
- You can't be successful.
- You don't deserve happiness.

Are you constantly questioning your worth and the words you say?

If you can relate to everything I've mentioned, your rejection wound needs acknowledging and healing.

How the rejection wound manifests in your relationships:

- You question yourself and think other people are more valuable than you.
- You may think you are too complicated, and that people aren't going to appreciate your opinions.

- Feeling rejected by your loved ones because you believe everything you do isn't good enough and any sign of distance from them means they don't love or appreciate you.
- You avoid getting close to others.
- You try and present yourself as untouchable because you're afraid to show your flaws.

The rejection wound can show up in your business as:

- Overthinking
- Avoiding growth
- Settling for less and playing small
- Stopping yourself from being visible online
- Stopping yourself from sharing your talents
- Procrastination
- Not feeling worthy of success
- The fear of becoming known by others

All of these things happen as a form of protection as our mind's priority is to protect us from harm.

How can you start healing your rejection wound?

Acknowledging where the rejection wound comes from.

You can track back to your childhood experiences and remember where the rejection stems from. There will also be events and emotions that you consciously won't remember until you work with your conscious and unconscious mind to get to the root cause via therapy. I do this with my clients using several different methods, including timeline therapy®,

Hypnotherapy, Rejection Wound™ Healing and Emotional Empowerment Coaching

Changing your internal programming.

The programming of your mind is currently built on many factors such as childhood experiences, your values, beliefs, memories and more. Healing is about unlearning old ways and learning new ways to think, feel and behave.

Accept and love yourself.

This isn't always easy, yet it becomes easier when you're on the road to recovery. All those years of carrying beliefs that weren't yours and the time and energy spent judging yourself can now be used to practise self-compassion, self-love and acceptance.

Your past does not define you. It can become a strength for your future self.

Stop your inner critic in its tracks.

We all have an inner critic. The inner critic is the voice within that puts us down usually with a positive intent to protect us from getting hurt and rejected

We also have another voice that is known as the soother or the nurturer. The voice of the inner critic may be recognised as a parent, carer, teacher or just an older version of you. Who it symbolises really doesn't matter because it's just a metaphorical representation of that person and nothing more.

Our unconscious mind stores things by creating a connection to things that have happened in the past. Both of these voices have a role to play in our lives. Our inner nurturer gives us self-compassion and love, whilst the inner critic helps you recognise where you may have gone wrong and what you need to do to set things right.

For most people, the inner critic goes over the top by constantly criticising and targeting them. It's like throwing dart after dart of naming, shaming, humiliating and finding faults. If it's big and powerful, while the inner nurturer is small and quiet, it will affect your self-esteem, self-worth and confidence.

The good news is, there are ways to reset this balance by restraining the critic and strengthening the nurturer inside yourself.

First, you need to observe how self-criticism operates inside you.

- Does it anger you?
- Do the thoughts of not being good enough creep up? Do you start dismissing any discomfort or your needs and your rights?
- Become aware of what happens internally when you achieve something: 'Oh, so what, anyone could have done that!', 'It wasn't all that anyway,' 'what about the other times when you messed up?'
- Observe any self-doubts and discouragement of your goals and dreams. When the inner critic starts going full force, I want you to know that your inner nurturer is a refuge and a safe voice to guide you and calm you down.

- Be aware of anger at yourself that seems out of proportion to what happened.
- Be mindful of your internal dialogue. Does it sound like scolding and shouting? You might notice some familiarity with the words, tone or attitude in the self-criticism, from your childhood. Does it remind you of anyone? A parent, sibling, relative, teacher? By listening to yourself, you can hear the harshness of what the inner critic has to say. Stepping back from the criticism to observe it can stop it reinforcing and help you to dis-identify from it. You may hear it, but you don't need to become it. This kind of calm witnessing can make the voice of your inner critic less intense and more reasonable.
- Argue against your inner critic, and truly intend to win. Think about someone who you feel is a good person. Someone you look up to. Then, think about someone else you consider to be a good person.
- Notice how often you see good qualities in others, even in people you don't know that well. Now turn it around and understand that those people are like you too, because what you see in others is a reflection of you.
- Recognise your own good qualities Recognise your good qualities and your talents them give them a label in your mind such as hard working; focused; or high achiever. Reassure yourself of how good you are at the things you love.
- Create a photo album in your phone of your achievement and all words and texts to describe the achievements. If you work with clients or customers, and they've given you good feedback and said positive

things about you, screenshot them and add them to that folder.
- Whenever the self-doubt and limiting beliefs creep up, remind yourself of what you have achieved before. As a result of significant emotional events, our mind creates limiting beliefs. Limiting beliefs are disempowering beliefs that hold us back from achieving our full potential.

Limiting beliefs keep us in our comfort zone. They can greatly limit and hinder our personal and professional goals. It is these thoughts, whether conscious or unconscious, that we regard as absolute truths. When you think a thought over and over again, it no longer remains a thought but becomes a belief. A limiting belief is something you believe all of the time even if it's in the back of your mind.

Every time you consciously attempt to make progress, the limiting beliefs in your unconscious mind will cause you to sabotage your success. By changing your thinking, you can change everything too.

I hope my chapter has been educational, inspirational and empowering. I pray you find healing, love and peace.

Feel free to reach out to me on my social media platforms if you require additional support.

Heal your rejection wound so you can set yourself free.

Much love,

Noshiela.

ABOUT THE AUTHOR
NOSHIELA MAQSOOD

Noshiela is a transformational Mindset, Emotional Empowerment Coach and NLP Trainer for women who has coached and trained women globally to create generational healing and change.

She is passionate about helping Muslim women heal their Rejection Wound so they can show up for their relationships and business with confidence and conviction.

She has coached and trained many women to heal and start their own profitable, passion-led coaching businesses. Creating a legacy of healed women, created generational change, one woman at a time.

13

UNCONDITIONAL

RAYNA PATTEE ISAACSON

> "Miracles begin with you; you must find the place inside yourself where nothing is impossible."
>
> — DEEPAK CHOPRA

"Let's go, let's go! Does everyone have their things? Water bottles, instruments, homework, lunches, backpacks, clean underwear on?" I hurriedly shouted reminders to everyone as I quickly usher them all into the car, praying they won't amass another tardy to their already impressive list of them.

As I open my car door and raise my leg to slide into the driver's seat, I notice something. There, perched precariously on the metal lip that rings the interior of the floor mat sits a penny. I pick it up and place it in my pocket. I grin and thank the heavens for what has become a familiar token left by those unseen around me.

Walking back into my home after school drop-off, I scan my

surroundings. My eyes instantly fall upon the kitchen and dining room. The main hub of our morning activity. I notice the half-eaten toast and abandoned cereal bowl. Left with six fruit loops encased in just enough milk to display their rainbow order. My daughter's crowning artistic achievement of the morning.

I see the silver cowboy boots that were hastily abandoned for a more sensible option for school. Wrinkled mounds of blankets were left out that were used by the early risers to keep warm while awaiting everyone to arise to the morning mayhem.

I start hurriedly picking up game boards that have been left out from the previous evening's entertainment, worried about the judgement or harsh criticism that I will hear when they are noticed. I stop and chide myself for slipping back into old patterns. Patterns and fear that no longer govern my life. I pause and breathe in the relief I feel. The relief of my newfound emotional freedom. I close my eyes and smile at the joy this liberation brings.

The moment is powerful but short as I hear my preschooler open the front door to let my daughter in. She is dropping off my granddaughter whom I tend to during the day while she's at work. I grab her some farm animals and graham crackers and place her down to watch television with my son.

They interact just like siblings. He quickly snatches her toy and hides it under her blanket as she crawls around in confusion. I take advantage of their beginning of the day camaraderie to look through my schedule that day. To quickly refamiliarize myself with the clients I will be meeting with.

Working is still such an odd reality for me. I'm consistently struck by the surrealness of my life. The career I never knew I always wanted growing and flourishing, while finishing out the one I've always had and loved. As I separated from my husband, I left financial security behind and built a career helping other women leave dysfunctional relationships and find their true path.

My life wasn't always this picturesque. The only vein of familiarity between these two lives are mess and chaos. I didn't feel joy anymore, at least not in my marriage.

I grew up as a member of the classic union between a narcissistic father and a codependent mother. I learned early on that negative attention was still attention. The "wrong crowd" quickly became my new tight knit family and I fell pregnant at age 15.

Through my own hard work, the help of many others, and many a blind eye from my teachers, I miraculously finished high school. Right after graduation I got a job at a bank. I dated some, but when you have a three-year old on your hip at age 18, the dating pool, as you might imagine, is sparse.

In my religion we believe that marriage is eternal. That families can be together forever. This is a truth I still cling to today. A truth that through cultural myths and my misunderstanding would keep me trapped in a marriage with someone I feared being in the same house with.

My husband checked the only box my ignorance and need to conform required. He was Mormon. My parents didn't like him and it felt like his parents didn't like me. Red flags that I should have paid attention to before we were married only nine months later.

We started as a family of three. And over the next twenty years, we would add eight more incredible children to the mix. I immediately acquired the titles of wife and stay-at-home mom. The latter has brought me the most joy and the most pain. It is what kept me caged for so many years. While I loved the role, it also kept me trapped.

Early on in my marriage, I could tell that something wasn't right. I had a small ache of emptiness at the bottom of my stomach. A small pang of unease that I learned early on to window dress with busyness. Raising as many young children as I had, I really was extremely busy, and the window dressing looked fabulous for all to see.

The small stomach pains struck with more intensity when I started to get frequent comments from friends like: "My husband would never speak to me like that." "Your husband sure is loud," or "Wow, your husband has quite the temper!" Yes, I started to recognize my marriage was quite different from those of my friends.

I would always laugh these comments off, and dismiss them. I was too proud to admit the similarities that I felt were emerging between my husband and my father, if I ever looked closely, I would silently applaud myself for being able to love someone with such rough edges. And I was going to do it for all of eternity!

Each anniversary I would carve another notch in my proverbial bedpost thinking how strong and dedicated a wife I was for holding in all the pain.

After close to two decades of living this way and becoming a mere shadow of my former self, the tint on my fancy rose-colored glasses began to wear off. I felt hollow and alone. I could no longer look past the growing angst I felt towards relationships and a religion I felt trapped by. Despite my best efforts, I was outgrowing this cage.

Thankfully, I'm a good actress. For me, the facade of a happy housewife was rather easy to portray. As you might imagine, when your house is a circus like mine, people get easily distracted by little things and rarely notice what lies just below the three-ringed surface. But beneath my happy house wife exterior, I was dying inside. I just couldn't quite place why. Between the emotional needs of my kids and what felt like a high maintenance marriage, I had a great distraction and excuse to ignore my own needs.

Looking over the last 25 years of my life feels like viewing someone else's life—A close relative maybe, but definitely not my own. Certainly, not my own. How was I able to fake it for so long, convince myself and the world all was good here?

I would crawl into bed every night exhausted, overwhelmed and more behind than when I had gotten up in the morning. Nights were filled with nursing babies and waking toddlers. Mornings started the rush, the laundry. Preparing dinner arrived all too soon, then bath time. Followed by utter exhaustion, crawling into bed only to have no sleep arrive. Rinse and repeat day after endless day.

Looking through much clearer lenses now I can see all the codependency traits I learned as a child playing out very nicely in my marriage. I was adept at notching that bedpost of martyrdom by doing everything. I allowed those around me to dictate my days. Everyone else's needs came way before my own. The codependency trait of people pleasing coursed through my veins.

I had grown up trying as best I could to control my environment in hopes of avoiding my father's terrifying rages. It was only natural for me to continue this in my marriage. I learned very early on that it was my job to make sure everything was perfect so that no one would feel stressed or lose their temper, and when they did, which was inevitable, it was clearly my fault for not doing enough.

My days passed trying to walk the thinnest of tightropes— Calming crying babies; keeping toddlers, magnets for exploration and adventure, from harming themselves and others; teaching children to read, write, wipe front to back and always wash their hands; helping kids navigate their emotions, always be kind and be a good friend; countless art activities; weekly outings; driving kids to and from school and to extracurricular activities, all the while meeting the every need of my husband.

The wonderful ups and downs of teenagers. Hormones, acne, drivers' licenses, school dances, jobs, dating and more broken hearts than I can count. Graduations, leaving the nest, weddings and grandchildren. You name it, I've seen it and probably helped someone through it. I loved being a stay-at-home mom and I was good at it. So good at it that I didn't have to acknowledge the unhealthy marriage I was in.

My husband was so good at providing financial support for the kids and me, that I felt showing gratitude for that meant dismissing and keeping silent about areas of concern I had. I didn't realize the cage it was actually building around me, and all of the things I sacrificed to stay in the comfort of that financial cage.

This all seems a million lifetimes ago. Many different versions of myself have evolved, so how could I feel so lost? Why was the pit in my stomach screaming so loudly that something wasn't right? I convinced myself I just needed to be more grateful for what a great provider my husband was, that allowed us all of these things. I just needed to work harder and do more so he would be happier.

The bar I felt had been set for me, that I never seemed to reach, was clearly caused by my deficit somewhere.

In 2015 my life was upended. I remember getting the phone call from my brother alerting me to the events that would so greatly alter my life's path. My father had suddenly and unexpectedly just passed away. I think that day will forever be etched into my memory bank. From the tears of disbelief to the pain of realizing the finality that came with my brother's announcement.

I remember clinging to the basket of laundry needing the comfort I found in the simple task of folding it. Craving the numbness only years of repeated movement could bring. It seemed about the only task I could undertake as my mind tried to reconcile the pain from the deep hole that had just been dug in my heart.

After my fathers passing I was forced to step away from the facade of perfection I had been so carefully crafting for the outside world and acknowledge my own feelings. That was a dark recognition. All of the wounds I had chosen to ignore from childhood were now screaming and demanding the attention I had been denying them for years.

Things were evolving and felt different. I felt my awareness of things growing. Interactions that I would usually dismiss to my own sensitivity I started to shed light on and became brave enough to ask my friends about their experiences in their own relationships.

Things I felt I was dismissing out of patience and love that would cause my friends to shutter and eyebrows to furrow in concern. Patterns I slowly started to learn were anything but normal.

Memories I had long since blocked of my parent's marriage were starting to appear. I started to see the strong similarities between my parent's marriage and my own. Similarities, causing the pit of unease in my stomach to grow.

The faint recollection of these memories always came after a fight between my husband and I. Fights that seemed to be increasing in number and frequency. Fights that were hours long. Circular arguing about the most trivial of things that left me utterly exhausted, emotionally drained, and me sobbing in my closet pleading to a God I felt had forsaken me. Feeling completely alone in a marriage where I felt unloved, unvalued, and unknown but bound to work things out because of my misunderstanding of eternity. Forced to work things out because no one was perfect and good people loved others despite their imperfections. We had nine children together. Physically speaking I had never been hit but emotionally I felt battered. How could it be that bad? It certainly must be me. I just needed to be more loving, giving and accepting. I was just too sensitive. I was the selfish one. I was the one that needed to change. The quiet moments I had with myself after these fights unearthed a very raw vulnerability within myself. One where I slowly started to realize I was not alone and that I most definitely needed to change. Just not in the way I thought.

In these quiet and raw moments, I was blessed with the opportunity to realize my heart was trying to speak to me along with someone else. The whisperings first began as small nudges of strength. They felt warm and distant, a knowing that I was ok. Each nudge came with some inner validation of truth towards some undeserved deficit in myself that my husband had tried to highlight in a fight.

With each nudge, I slowly started to chip away at a false reality that I felt had been built around me regarding my character. I started to awaken to different strengths and truths I possessed I had been told weren't true. These quiet nudges didn't come all the time. They were rather sporadic, but the more I started to pay attention to them the more they came. Along with these nudges and random memories of my parent's marriage, I would strangely also have fleeting memories from my childhood come to the surface.

I don't have many memories of my childhood. There are very few that pop up organically on their own. The ones I have after looking through photo books I can't tell if they are contrived or real. A truth my brain is recalling or just something it is reconfiguring to plug a hole. The memories that came to mind always came with this overwhelming feeling of sorrow, but not my own.

One night after a particularly ugly fight that had left me reeling with uncertainty and sadness, I started to piece things together. I started to recognize the origin of my slow awakening.

"Dad?!?!" I cried in a moment where I clearly thought I had truly lost it.

The answer I received wasn't anything made for cinematic suspense. No doors slammed shut or lights flickered off. I just felt an overwhelming peace and loving connection no earthly words can properly illustrate, and so my new relationship with my dad began posthumously.

This new relationship wasn't built over shared bowls of ice cream, strolls through the park or bonding over similar likes in pop culture. It grew out of uncertainty, lots of self-doubt, and relearning how to trust.

My father started highlighting unhealthy patterns in my marriage but most importantly unhealthy patterns in myself. I started to recognize my own insecurities and doubts I had about myself that allowed me to tolerate people mistreating me.

Steven Chbosky wrote it best:

> "We accept the love we think we deserve."

The powerlessness I felt towards my fathers rages and the people it harmed had left me with a belief that I wasn't good enough to be loved. I learned to love difficult people and tolerate their cruel treatment because their love, as toxic as it was, was all I deserved.

There are many flaws in this thinking, the worst being questioning our worthiness. I had been raised in a home and then walked straight into a marriage where I felt love was conditional. A flaw in my thinking I could feel my father desperately trying to undo.

If you had asked me six years ago what unconditional love was, my response would have been very different from the one I believe today. A definition crafted and chiselled in my heart changing through all the different versions of me over the years.

Unconditional. Merriam Webster describes this as:

> "not subject to any conditions."

The two words it gives after the definition to describe it are "absolute" and "unqualified". I love the use of these two words in this definition. I love the strong solidarity of the word absolute and the comforting forgiveness the word unqualified provides. I love that the two words used in this definition started to match all my father was teaching me about it. Not just towards others, but towards myself.

I could feel my father's sorrow for how he had acted on Earth, and I could also feel the true him - what I think of as his higher self. I was actually feeling and internalizing, how he wished he could have been, and how he was now. I could feel how much he loved me. Then, now and always. Unconditionally. It was a constant. Like the rose-colored glasses I wore for so many years, all the human constraints we experience muck up this beautiful reality.

The firm reality of unconditional love transcending this earthly realm started to open my eyes to a new way of seeing my days. I now saw the belief systems I had built around blurred lenses and human frailty that I was perpetuating in my own children.

I was able to recognize that I had been viewing religion and relationships all wrong - especially the one I had with myself. I had been operating from a belief that I had to earn love - God's love, my parents' love, love from community, family, friends and especially from a spouse.

Thinking that I had failed to earn my father's love and his mine before he died, I was completely blown open by my father's death. Knowing now how wrong I had been and how loved I was, has changed everything.

I had spent so many years in the shadow of victimhood. It made so much sense, and I had so much evidence to support why I felt unloved, lost and defeated, I never stopped to question why I was choosing that, or that someone could be manipulating me into and counting on me choosing that. Once I started entering my days choosing to believe I was loved, and not alone, my life changed.

The more I started recognizing my dad's love and presence the more other angelic help made itself known. I started feeling this huge network of divine guidance surrounding me and my family. Some were presences I had never met in the earthly realm. Some were individuals I had only met once and had been deceased for over twenty years.

Our communication just came as sort of an odd sense of just knowing. I could feel their personalities. I could feel their strengths and sorrows. I started to understand the familiarities and why certain ones chose to stand sentinel over my children to guide them through their darkest hours.

Luckily I had been fortunate enough to have started this journey with angels before the nightmare of 2020 and the pandemic turned the world upside down. No one was left unscathed by this experience, least of all my family.

My mother joined my angel network. We gathered all of our children and their significant others home to weather the unknown. Our home now had 13 people, two dogs and two cats. Six of my children were still in school which was now taught at home.

My husband's job, which pre-pandemic had him travelling two weeks out of every month, now had him home 24/7. The cracks in our marriage that we had been able to ignore were now completely exposed.

However, I was stronger. I knew I was loved and supported. I was starting to outgrow the cage of conditional love I felt had built around me. I was realizing that true and healthy relationships are not built on conditions.

This was not, though, a linear process. There were days I still felt trapped, held in place by religious leaders telling me to pray for change and the bleak outlook any stay at home mom is met with when viewing her options for supporting herself.

There were times that I started back in my old patterns of thinking: *If I was more righteous things would be better. I was too sensitive; that's why I was miserable.* I fervently prayed for change.

In the end, the change didn't come from others. It came from me.

I started focusing intently on love—pure, unconditional love. I would make a conscious choice every morning to stop operating from the confines of a cage of conditions and just trust love. I just chose to choose love. It was as simple and hard as that.

My main objective became for those around me to know how much I loved them. Unconditionally. If those I came in contact with could feel my love for them, maybe it wouldn't be so hard for them to feel the greater love they had around them from God and their angels.

This was hard. I had to focus inward and shed light on some pretty dark corners of my heart. I had to quit relying on my familiar responses and defense mechanisms and examine my role in how I could be contributing to hurt feelings. I listened to podcast after podcast. Read book after book. My quest for knowledge and growth was insatiable.

In talking to people about all of the things I was learning and processing I noticed a career path starting to form in front of me. I loved viewing the world with my new clear lenses and I was really good at helping other women trapped in the shadows of their own dark marriage, and realize they were loved and not alone either.

Through the years I spent in the fog of abuse I had become very adept at communicating with a narcissist. I was very good at deciphering the many verbal tactics they employ to control their supply, and I was becoming very good at helping other women to see and understand when it was being used on them. I helped them carefully craft responses while their own fog lifted. I started adding different coaching certifications to my database and toolkit of knowledge. I was growing, unconditionally.

Certain days felt like my head and shoulders were emerging from my cage. Most days, fear and self doubt still kept most of me trapped within. The difference now was that I wasn't just outgrowing my cage. I wanted out of my cage. I wanted reinvention and transformation. I just had to start trusting that I could do it.

I was sitting in a coach mastery training when I first realized I could do it. I had spent a week of sitting in a room with 100 other women being taught and coached, every day from 9-5. The goal, along with learning, was for each woman to be publicly coached at least once. This served the purpose of learning what it was like to be coached and how to coach.

I sat back and soaked a lot in that week. That week affirmed a lot. I knew this material. I was a good coach.

The biggest lesson came from when I was the one being coached. I came knowing exactly what I needed coaching on, but never raised my hand because I also knew what would be said. I was terrified to confront the truth.

I sat and watched person after person be coached day after day. It was the last day and I was the last person. The coach asked what I wanted coaching on. I said I knew I needed to tell my husband I wanted a divorce but was too scared. She asked what the worst thing that could happen was. Her look of horror and lack of response at my answer, taught me a lot that day.

People in healthy relationships don't understand the trauma that comes from abuse that is covert and hidden. They unknowingly gaslight women into thinking that because they aren't hit, they aren't being abused.

Leaders in my church, in healthy relationships, were especially guilty of this. Trapping women in an abusive relationship because of their faith. Women in emotionally and verbally abusive relationships needed a special kind of voice and I realized that day I was able to be that voice.

I slowly started to accept clients. I loved helping women wake up to the cage around them and wake up to the simple key they possessed to unlock their confines, but I felt like a fraud. I still felt trapped, kept stuck in my own cage by fear and self doubt. Until one magical day I realized the piece I had been leaving out.

I was away on the very first trip I had ever planned and taken by myself. I had decided I was worth my dreams and decided to attend a workshop conducted by one of my heroes. Here I had the opportunity to be looked in the eyes by him and told I was worth it.

When you've gone your whole life never hearing this phrase and then being told this by someone you revere it sheds old beliefs. I left that workshop feeling whole.

On the last day of my trip, I was sitting on the beach. I received a phone call that instantly drew me back into my cage. I hung up my phone and walked into the water until my feet were immersed in the calming ebb and flow of the waves.

I started sobbing and yelling out to God, my angels, the universe. Whoever was there to listen. I cursed them for still being stuck in my cage and pleaded to know I would be ok if I left it. I was ready to jump off my proverbial cliff, I just needed to know someone would catch me. "Please let me know!" I prayed the hardest I'd ever prayed for a sign that day.

I asked to see a whole sand dollar. I needed to see a whole sand dollar. I immediately started to apologize and doubt my hasty demand but started scouring the beach in desperation too.

After a few minutes a sand dollar floated up only to be instantly reclaimed by the ocean. I cursed my angels, told them that they needed to do better than that and immediately started looking again. Same thing. A whole sand dollar floated to me, and in an instant was drawn back out.

By this time I am sobbing, wondering how I will ever survive, when I am seized by a moment of hope and recognition. I yelled out, "DAD!!! I know you are there! I know you can do this! I know it! Please! I need you to do this! I need to see a whole sand dollar! PLEASE!"

Through eyes blurred with fear, skepticism and tears I start to scour the beach one last time. Two minutes later an entirely intact sand dollar gently floats up and rests on the arch of my foot. I stare at it in disbelief and then I quickly snatch it up and start sobbing in gratitude and reassurance.

Not one minute later a second one floats up as well. A bonus one. I know instantly that this is a token of my mom's faith in me. A sign to walk a path she was never brave enough too. "Thanks mom" I say as I look like a mad woman walking home along the beach sobbing and talking to what seems like herself.

Those two sand dollars encompassed all of the truths I had been forgetting and leaving out of my coaching. Not only do we need to awaken to the strength and power that is within us, but we also need to awaken to the strength and the power that is all around us in the form of ancestral angels that love us and want us to be the end to the generations of abuse they and us have endured and tolerated. Those sand dollars were more than tokens of hope. They were tokens of love, trust and guidance on a path I have been placed on to help others like me.

Wayne Dyer said: "If you knew who walked beside you at all times on the path that you have chosen, you could never experience fear or doubt again." It wasn't until I embraced this that I learned how to bring spiritual awareness to others that transcends any religious denomination.

It allows me to teach women how to connect with their inner self and the spiritual world for grounding and guidance while expertly helping them navigate the day to day necessary communications with their partner, regardless of whether they are in or out of the relationship.

Some relationships are salvageable. They are able to be deconstructed and rebuilt without conditions and toxicity. Some aren't. That's not up to me to decide. My passion is to help women awaken to their true selves. Awaken to the light within and around them. Rediscover their power, their purpose and what makes them feel alive.

We are loved and we are not alone. It's my purpose to help women realize this and awaken to the strength this small concept can bring, and the power it has in helping them attain the life of their dreams.

ABOUT THE AUTHOR
RAYNA PATTEE ISAACSON

Rayna helps women awaken to the angelic love and support that is constantly around them, while also awakening them to their own light and power within.

Before starting a coaching business, Rayna was a stay at home mom of 9 children and 1 grand baby, her most beloved and educational job. Mothering and unconditionally loving 9 vastly different spirits through the storms of life has brought her more wisdom and knowledge to help in her coaching career than any formal education she has bought.

Rayna has specialized as a Narcissistic Trauma and Abuse Coach, that is trauma informed, helping women heal the unseen wounds that emotionally and verbally abusive relationships leave. She has also worked as a High Conflict Divorce Coach and Dream Big Coach. Rayna loves helping women come full circle on their healing journey and moving into a life of purpose and embracing their full potential.

Rayna is a strong member of The Church of Jesus Christ of Latter Day Saints and has helped many women awaken to the love God has for them after they have felt forsaken, punished and alone in their relationships.

On Rayna's dream days you will find her on the beach, in the mountains or on some grand adventure with her children. Rayna enjoys sarcastic humor, well placed swear words and would never turn down a proposal from John Wick.

Rayna is available for 1:1 coaching, group coaching and speaking engagements.

Rayna can be reached at:

TheWomensAwakeningCoach@gmail.com

TheWomensAwakeningCoach.com

She is also starting a podcast, "Ray of Light" found anywhere you listen to podcasts.

- facebook.com/thewomensawakeningcoach
- instagram.com/thewomensawakeningcoach
- tiktok.com/@thewomensawakeningcoach

14

RELEASING PAIN TO FIND PEACE: A WELLNESS JOURNEY

REBECCA MITCHELL

I START TODAY WITH GRATITUDE. I AM THANKFUL AND I FEEL peaceful. Sitting at my kitchen table, with a glass of water, I can hear the birds outside and feel the breeze drifting in through my open doors, connecting me to nature.

I feel connected to everything around me. I am regulated and calm as I think about my 'past life' and my struggles in traumatic events. I can feel how important it was for me to release the pain that was both in my mind and somatically held in my body. It has been incredible to create my life-changing programme, The Wellness Steps, which aims to support introverted women who feel isolated or lost take easy steps on a healthy journey back to a well-balanced and happy life.

It feels a great privilege to encourage women, just like me, to take positive steps to move forward, to break out of feelings of isolation, being disconnected or feeling unworthy. To be able to support survivors of trauma, narcissistic trauma, divorce and significant life events.

This calmness and connection I feel is a million miles away from where I used to be! Where I feel peace now, I felt chaos then; where I feel connected now, I felt loneliness then; where I feel happiness now, I felt hurt; where I feel healthy now, I felt rundown; where I look forward to tomorrow now, I felt I couldn't go on then...

It is hard to write those words and not feel the emotion of reliving the moments in a time of being so low.

And as much as I can now see a clearer, wider view: finding out about the affair that destroyed my family felt at the time to be the single most devastating moment.

Everything I thought I knew changed. I felt betrayed, my four young children let down and it was a pivotal life-changing event as I went through a very painful separation and difficult divorce.

During this time I found Caroline Strawson online. I feel fortunate to have met Caroline because she helped me understand that this happened to me and not because of me. Those are important words to hear because when you give everything you can, where you are all about your family, and then that life you thought you were living isn't true, the world literally crashes down around you and you are unsure what is reality.

Through working with Caroline, I mapped out a trauma timeline which showed significant events from when I was born until now. It was eye-opening and a revelation as I realised while there were events in my life that had been extremely difficult emotionally, and there were a lot of them, I had managed to find ways to cope and move forward, yet my body was still holding on to the pain.

It was such an important piece of work that it formed the basis of the *Wellness Steps*. My mission is to support real life health awareness for women understanding and overcoming the effects of trauma.

So what does a trauma timeline look like? In simple terms, take a piece of paper and start to map out where significant events happened in your life. It could be anything over your entire life that has caused you to feel emotional distress: your parents divorce, a sibling being taken to hospital, living with domestic abuse as an adult. What is a trauma to one person may not be viewed as a trauma to another, therefore this is an individual exercise to understand what shaped who you are.

This process is cathartic, but can be triggering, and I have guided many people safely through this process. What begins to emerge is a unique biography of you! And to see these wounds mapped out shows the strength we have inside, and where our brains have protected us.

To illustrate what I mean, I am now going to draw out three significant trauma wounds on my timeline, how I survived them and moved forward.

On New Years Eve, 2011, one of my daughters was born with an undiagnosed, potentially fatal condition, which was only discovered at birth during an emergency C-Section.

That was a traumatic birth throughout. I remember the most horrendous pain in my shoulders and my struggle to breathe, where the anaesthetist had to intervene.

When my daughter was born to our world, she was briefly shown to me, and then she was taken away. I was moved to a room with curtains pulled shut all around, and the doctor explained what he thought it was, with a book in his hand - in all my pain, relief and shock I remember his kindness, but the words 'tumour' and 'possibly cancerous' were difficult to process. My daughter was rushed by ambulance from the maternity hospital to a paediatric hospital.

Nothing prepared me for having a seriously ill child. I was discharged from the maternity hospital the next day after having my c-section and was admitted to the paediatric hospital to be with my daughter. I can look back to my younger adult self and see how ill I was. On autopilot after my operation and desperate to make sense of my daughter's condition, my own needs were instinctually lowered to insignificant. I can even feel those emotions now in my body, trying to cope with the news about my tiny daughter. In writing this now I feel like I would like to put my arms around my younger self and say everything will be alright.

My daughter's tumour was removed when she was twelve days old, and they removed her tailbone to prevent recurrence. She has been monitored by the hospital regularly since then with ultrasounds and blood tests to keep her safe and healthy and ensure that the tumour does not return. There was a possibility that she wouldn't walk properly, and/or have bladder and bowel problems.

It was really hard to process, and as an introverted woman, I felt alone trying to navigate what this meant for my daughter. I found a community online with parents and families of children like my daughter while I was searching for help and answers; and I also found that many babies don't make it through pregnancy as the tumour grows. It was, and still is, a community I felt connected to and I shared the beautiful wins and tragic losses of these wonderful children and their amazing parents. This supportive community understood what I was going through, where friends and family did not, and I have gratitude for this incredible group.

In recent times, when my daughter has a follow-up appointment, or indeed any childhood appointments, I am asked for her date of birth. As a New Years Eve baby, or Hogmanay baby in Scotland, it is a significant day. A comment like 'that must have been a big party', where I nod and say 'Yes' is an example of how we cover up our difficult emotional events and traumas. It is important that we recognise these moments and do not suppress these events, which stay embedded in our bodies. It is important to know that while some do not understand, there are those who do understand.

Another 'significant life event' I will highlight from my trauma timeline, was the sad death of my wonderful father in 2015.

It was a ten year-long journey my dad had with prostate cancer, and for that final year I would attend the specialist clinic with him for his appointments. He participated in several clinical trials to further research cures for cancer, in alignment of who he was and to make a difference to others.

My Dad was a secondary school English and Learning Support teacher by profession and a talented sportsman and music enthusiast with his hobbies. He was immersed in music and loved exploring new bands on the scene. He was a doting father to his three daughters and loving grandad to his little grandchildren.

I was with my Dad when he passed away. He received the best care as his body gave way to Prostate Cancer, and suffered two strokes in his last month with us. My sisters and I took turns staying overnight so he was never alone. He would sometimes wake in a start and then he would see me and his eyes would smile as they locked on me and they would close softly again to rest.

I cry as I recall this moment: when my wonderful Dad was taking his final breaths I was holding his hand and he could feel my touch and I could tell him I was there and that he was ok. And he was not alone.

Grief can be a lonely, hidden experience. I was thirty-five when I lost my dad, and after his funeral and my sisters and I were back at our homes to get on with our lives again, I realised that I didn't know anyone close to me who had gone through losing a parent. It is hard to talk about because it is unbearable to think about not seeing your loved one again. One moment you can be fine and the next, you can be sobbing uncontrollably. It was hard to speak to my sisters because we would all cry. And therefore we started avoiding talking about the injustice of it all. We each tried to deal with it within.

With no one to talk to, feelings of guilt like wishing I had spent more time with him crept in and overshadowed the brilliant things we did together. My sisters and I went to New York with my dad for his 70th birthday the year before he died. It was just before he took part in a clinical trial and we fitted it in just in time. I feel happy thinking of being away with him and we have that connection with him always.

Yet the overwhelming feelings of grief are not forgiving and are difficult to live with, which is why using connection therapy to make connections with those experiencing similar situations, and connecting with positive memories of passed loved ones are such a significant process.

Getting out of my house and being in the open air, next to water and being away from the constricts of a building helped me work through my feelings. There is something unique about being present in nature which is a healing experience.

The other 'difficult experience' I will refer to from my trauma timeline is in 2021 and the diagnosis of autism for my son, then aged four, and my research to understand, leading to a battle for support and to find practical approaches for the family.

I felt isolated in trying to understand how to help my son in his developmental milestones.

"Boys are different"... "my son couldn't speak until he was four"... "he looks absolutely fine"... "I wish my son didn't talk, it's just non-stop"...

I will always appreciate the sentiment from friends, yet there is the sixth sense that as a parent, that as a parent there seems to be something else. There was no one to really talk to about my feelings because others want to cure or minimise the worries.

Having gone through the mental struggles of possible physical challenges and disability with my daughter five years before, it was a completely different mental struggle navigating a hidden disability, such as autism, with my son.

I found supportive groups, where I could learn more and celebrate wins with other parents. It is helpful to be surrounded by a global community of people who understand and are online, just a moment away.

Releasing Pain to Find Peace: A Wellness Journey

In Covid Lockdown, I was fortunate that my son was given a vulnerable child space to attend Nursery when they reopened. Sometimes we don't realise the angels are right in front of us carrying their wisdom and knowledge to help us through hard times. At other times we have to fight really hard to find them as we navigate paperwork, continually being moved from person to person and department to department.

The forms I had to fill in to support my son's disability were difficult. At times I could hardly face it. Yet as a mother of a special needs child, I had to find the inner strength to keep going, to make the phone calls, to ask the difficult questions again and again - for him. My son started his mainstream school journey in August 2022, after being deferred a year, and continues to grow as my very special blessing.

As I was able to explore my timeline visually, going back forty years, taking a step back, I was seeing myself living through many significant, emotional events and some really difficult times. I held a lot of pain in my nervous system as well as psychologically. I cry as I think of the times I cried on my own.

I would like to put my arms around my younger self and say 'it's not easy, I'm proud of you'.

The words "this happened to you, not because of you" once again are important here because we can each carry a lot of guilt and shame with us. This pressure is in our bodies and pressure is in our minds.

I realised if my trauma timeline was flipped to create a *Vertical Trauma Timeline*, with me at the bottom holding it on my shoulders, it becomes easy to see how much pressure is sitting there, weighing me down. Pressure and weight that is carried around every day and all of these life-changing events make up who we are.

These pressures have emotional attachments and as mentioned the impact of coping with grief, for example, that may appear any day unexpectedly. We are all walking about with our own *Vertical Trauma Timeline*, with that pressure on our shoulders.

One such trauma, which we all share in our timelines, is the significant event of living in Lockdown.

This was a different experience for all of us. I have friends who lost loved ones, who lost their business, who struggled with the expectation of working at home with small children, continued going to work as a key worker in accommodation away from their family and friends and who dealt with the grief and pain of comforting strangers as they passed away in hospital without their family.

These recollections are unimaginably painful. They are held somatically in our bodies and emotionally in our minds.

Lockdown is definitely a pivotal moment on my timeline. The sudden isolation amplified all of my feelings and my situation. At home with four children, two who need to be home-schooled, my three year old autistic son and my active two year old daughter was extremely challenging.

Some of us connected more with our children, spent more time outside in nature, created Zoom quiz nights with friends and family, or did fitness classes in our living rooms. These examples of connections we made to other people, nature and ourselves is what helped navigate us through that unexpected and isolating event, and demonstrates how powerful connections can be.

This is the beginning where the *Wellness Steps* formed. I realised that through the connections I make with others, nature and myself I am able to release my pain and find peace. My awareness was that each of us is balancing our own *Vertical Trauma Timeline* on our shoulders as well as in our minds and trying to keep on with our lives at the same time. When observing other people's trauma experiences I could see that the same connections would help them too.

We are all made up of our own significant events and they have shaped who we are. We are all different, we all look at life through different eyes. If we looked at each other through a trauma-informed lense, we would come to realise that we are all trying our best based on our background and experiences where our beliefs are formed.

We all have trauma within us and we all have the ability to get ourselves back on track with support, knowledge and making informed decisions.

So I immersed myself in bringing together all of the knowledge I had acquired to support other people to become connected again in these three important areas. Connection to People, Connection to Nature and Connection to Ourselves.

I am a *Brainspotting Practitioner and Certified Narcissistic Trauma Coach*, which enables me to get to the root of locked trauma and support a healthy journey to wellness with mind and body. My experience as a national Education and Training Strategist, and using my health, wellness and holistic background, gave me a unique overview to develop an overall embodied journey.

The Wellness Steps starts with understanding who an individual is, by understanding the brain and body. Working together, specific techniques are appropriately chosen to help regulate using the five senses to be connected to Self, for example proven breathing or tapping exercises. And only then we begin mapping a *Vertical Trauma Timeline.* An example is: use Brainspotting Therapy for deep healing and to release trapped trauma, working on connection to self, community and nature, then map out how we can use methods such as nutrition and aromatherapy for wellness. I use a Steps method as some days we can feel in 'freeze mode' and other days are raring to go, and so all options are considered and available to support individual experiences for people like you and me on their healing journey.

There are four inspiring women I would like to introduce you to, who have worked with me and worked on their Wellness Steps through Connection to People, Connection to Nature and Connection to Ourselves.

Stephanie is a 49 year old mum, who is divorced and through the breakdown of her marriage had lost friends, felt isolated, had put on weight, felt shame and embarrassment about life turning out as it had. We worked together to identify her *Vertical Trauma Timeline* and we put in place a Wellness Programme, with some specific Divorce Coaching. We teased out what made her feel happy, and where to support a better and achievable nutritious shopping basket to help her become well from the inside out. We set out the steps to her wellness.

Using Brainspotting, we pinpointed the isolation she felt, and we made small steps at a time to move forward at her pace. Stephanie is living a more connected life after joining a local walking club. Through the connections she made there, she joined a Wild Sea Swimming group. Her connection to people, nature and her senses has turned her life around. Her smile radiates through her eyes.

Tasnim is a 41 year old survivor of trauma in childhood. In adulthood, she escaped the trauma of a narcissistic marriage. To protect her children, she faced the harsh reality of being re-traumatised going through the Family Courts. She had been financially abused and relying on foodbanks, and was at a really low point.

After using her senses to feel connected to herself, with breathwork, tapping and aromatherapy, we carefully worked on her *Trauma Timeline* and used *Brainspotting* to work through her trapped trauma. She had been estranged from her family through her abusive marriage and yet through the *Wellness Steps* she gradually re-connected in small steps. We took time to realign her belief system and rebuild positive habits to bring comfort and happiness day-to-day. As part of the Wellness Community, Tasnim now has people around her that understand her, motivate her and listen to her. Tasnim has a positive outlook on what she can control in her life.

Rachel is a 62 year old retired teacher and grandmother, suffering from Long Covid and caring for her husband who tragically suffered a stroke. She felt overweight and was drinking too much. We worked together on changing habits and breaking the habit of alcohol use to cope and as a reward. We used Brainspotting, which enabled Rachel to understand her feelings of isolation and injustice, and also validated her journey.

A nutrition programme supported Rachel's wellness and was one of the greatest contributors to her connection to herself and her health has improved incredibly. Both breathing and tapping exercises worked well for Rachel to support her situation. The new energy she gained gave her the boost to meet up with friends again instead of avoiding seeing other people. Rachel's responsibilities as a carer and grandmother are the same, yet her energy and connection is allowing her to now live a fulfilled life.

Tina, 28, was working hard as a City Accountant. She felt very unappreciated, had really low self-esteem and had continuous feelings of not being good at anything; she felt immensely burned out. Through Brainspotting, we pinpointed that Tina had been working in an abusive workplace, with senior managers that communicated inappropriately and had put a lot of pressure and expectation on her with little acknowledgement. Tapping and aromatherapy worked well for Tina and she uncovered she was a people-pleaser, and had been taken advantage of. We used steps to ensure Tina was working safely, and she began applying for new jobs to connect to people that appreciated her. She joined an Art Class a short drive away, which led to volunteering in a beach-cleaning group and has built new friendships with like-minded people. She is now thriving, with a new job, new connections, being outside with nature and making time for herself with healthy choices to support her journey to Wellness.

These inspiring women were carrying significant pressures, not realising they had experienced traumatic events, held in both their bodies and their minds. The last priority uncovered was being themselves. By separating out what they are in control of and what they are not in control of, and how they can regulate and respond, these women could start taking steps at their own pace towards healing and living a more positive and fulfilled life.

Releasing Pain to Find Peace: A Wellness Journey

Using the *Wellness Steps* philosophy of Connection to People, Connection to Nature and Connection to Ourselves at our own pace, with our own lifestyle in mind is a natural journey to support different stages of recovery and wellness for all individuals to address the weight of our *Vertical Trauma Timeline*.

We are all connected, and I feel honoured to be able to support women through their journey and taking the steps to change and move forward using my proven technique.

I would like to finish as I started with gratitude and thank you for reading my story of finally being able to release pain and take steps forward for healing. This is a journey and not a destination, yet I am confidently equipped to live a happy and fulfilled life no matter what I can or cannot control.

I have immense thankfulness and an innate sense of inner peace and calm that I will carry forward and treasure as I feel the breeze on my skin and a comforting feeling of connection.

ABOUT THE AUTHOR
REBECCA MITCHELL

Rebecca is passionate about supporting introverted women, who feel isolated or lost through separation or divorce, to take steps on a healthy journey back to a well-balanced and happy life.

From her background as a National Education and Training strategist and using proven techniques from experience and extensive training, Rebecca created the Wellness Steps, a holistic and life-changing programme.

This includes Vertical Trauma Timeline Therapy, Mind and Body Therapy and Three Pillars of Connection: to People, to Nature and Ourselves. Rebecca is degree qualified and is a Brainspotting Practitioner, Trauma and Wellness Coach and Narcissistic Abuse Specialist.

Living in the West of Scotland, and mum to four lively children, Rebecca is also an enthusiastic volunteer Girls' Football Coach, providing opportunities for girls to engage in sports and health outdoors, have fun and make new friends. "If we can give strength, health, community and opportunities to girls, we are positively supporting their prospects as strong, healthy and connected women".

Rebecca is available for 1:1 and Group Coaching, contact:

Email - thewellnesssteps@gmail.com

'The Wellness Steps' App is available from your App Store, and Rebecca's podcast 'The Wellness Steps' for introverted women is available November 2022, on all platforms.

facebook.com/thewellnesssteps
instagram.com/thewellnesssteps

15

FEEDING THE WOLF

VALERIE SUSSMAN, MD.

A Babe in the Woulds (How Much is that Wolfie in the Window?)

> "Well-behaved women seldom make history."
>
> — LAUREL THATCHER ULRICH

This is a story of a would-be wolf woman (i.e. me), who *unwilded* herself to placate and please others.

She disowned and disavowed her hungers, her passions, and her prowesses. She abandoned the wild woods of her intuition and knowing for the penned-in pastures of others' expectations. She discounted her value and underestimated her worth as a wolf, shapeshifting herself to become a shorn sheep, a sacrificial lamb, window dressing for the big bad wolf.

Eventually she learned (the hard way, of course), that self-sacrifice is too steep a price for a she-wolf-to-be.

A wild wolf woman will not be silenced forever.

Pups, Dogs, and Watered-Down Wolves

I was born a wolf. Like all pups, I was spirited, rambunctious, uninhibited, and expressive. I spent a good bit of my early days upside down, flipping and flopping and cartwheeling in the gym or on any long stretch of grass or sand. I played basketball with the guys, who on occasion would actually throw me the ball. And, yes, I spent too many hours of my junior high days sitting in the hall outside the classroom, banished for being too social, too animated, too feisty.

I was curious, courageous, and goofy. I was creative. I was a wolf on her way.

Then Hermie came along. Let me introduce you to my old friend, Hermie: *'Hermie's Hot Dog Stand'* was a short story I wrote for Mrs. Grayson's seventh grade English class. Oh, was I proud of *'Hermie!'*

The story went like this: Hermie was the proud owner of a hot dog stand, predictably named *'Hermie's Hot Dog Stand.'* Hermie's hot dogs were world-renowned. People came from miles around to partake of these scrumptious delights. These hot dogs were *good*. Unfortunately, one day, the hot dog stand was robbed at gunpoint. The kicker? The robber did not want Hermie's money; he wanted the hot dogs. The coup de gras in this masterpiece of seventh grade fiction was the oh-so-clever line, *'Hand over the wieners and no one gets hurt!'*

Not surprisingly, Mrs. Grayson was not nearly as impressed with this grand opus as was my twelve-year-old self, and the grade I received reflected this. So, good student that I was, I shut down my goofiness. I shut down my creativity. The cartwheels and the flipping stopped. I re-righted my upside-down self. I became a good little pup. I sat, I stayed, I lied down, I silenced, I played dead.

'*Good girl,*' the they-wolves said.

I stopped trusting my instincts, my inner knowing, deferring instead to the '*alphas*' in the pack for instructions on how to be a well-behaved woman in this world. I performed and I conformed. I pleased and I appeased. The wolf pup in me was put out to pasture. I had shape-shifted into a freshly shorn sheep.

I was a *good girl*.

Who Let the Wolves In? ("The Calls are Coming from Inside the House")[1]

> "No one can make you feel inferior without your consent."
>
> — ELEANOR ROOSEVELT

The role and goal of a good sheep is to follow, to fit in with the flock. Do not rock the boat, do not upset the apple cart.

I had cast out my inner me-wolf so that I could follow the leaders. As I let my own wolf out, I let the other wolves in. I fully cooperated as I was de-fanged, de-clawed, and de-howled. Their *shoulds* became my *shoulds*. I adopted and enshrined their ideas of who I was and their aspirations for who I was to become. I played small. I shrank to fit into my now-sleepy sheepy life. These they-wolves embedded themselves and their agendas into my psyche.

Boundaries? What boundaries? I had internalized the predators.

The hits kept coming:

'Smile. You'll look so much prettier.' - Questionably well-intended random strangers to my teenaged self, apparently ignorant of the well-known fact that moody, hormonal teenagers do *not* walk around smiling. The hit? I felt flawed. And ugly.

'You're not skinny enough, and… gasp!... Is that cellulite?'—Me, definitely not well-intended, catching my reflection, apparently ignorant of the fact that teenagers do *not* walk around feeling skinny. The hit? I felt fat. And ugly.

'Go to medical school and become a doctor'—My parents and teachers, likely well-intended, who had seemingly decided on my career choice without consulting me. The hit? I felt dominated. (Although, they at least wanted me to be a doctor, not just marry one—I was a good student, remember?)

'What do you mean, you got a 'B'?! You'll never get into medical school with a 'B'!' —My father, well-intended, but a bit overly demanding. The hit? I felt diminished. (Note: I got into medical school *and* I became a doctor— I was a good girl.)

'You're wearing fleece again?'—My sweatpants-allergic, image-conscious ex-husband, apparently unaware of the fact that I was a sheep. (Definitely not well-intended.) The hit? I felt unloved. And ugly—again.

'Sheep up or ship out!'— My internalized predators. (Ok, I made this one up, but it was an ongoing refrain in my head.)

Who let the wolves in? I did.

Who let my me-wolf out?

Me again.

That's the hit.

Ouch.

In the Belly of the Wolf (What Big Teeth)

When I first met my ex-husband I was captivated. I was hooked. I was consumed. He was handsome, funny, smart, charismatic, energetic. He was considerate, complimentary, and supportive. My prince was charming. He was disarming. Until he wasn't.

My prince, in time, revealed himself to be critical, demeaning, cold, withholding, selfish, passive-aggressive, entitled. Perhaps not so charming?

In fact, he was *harming*.

I went from captivated to captive. It turns out, I had chosen a narcissist, a.k.a. a *wolf in sheep's clothing*.

And… it was I who had let him in.

'The calls are coming from inside the house.' [1](Fuck.)

Still-Life on the Ranch: A-Sheep at the Wheel

Meanwhile, back at the ranch… this white-washed would-be-wolf, a.k.a. sheep, decided to make a life with the would-be prince. Yes, I wedded the wolf. (Sigh.)

What happens when an over-giver meets an over-taker?

Well… I spent twenty years a-sheep at the wheel of this wolf. I played beta to his alpha. On occasion I did try to backseat-drive. I whimpered, even growled, but mostly only succeeded in backseat-driving myself to exhaustion. Nevertheless, I sat. I stayed. I lied down. I rolled over. I played dead. Emotionally I *was* dead. I tried to keep up with the increasing demands of this hungry, angry wolf. (Can you say, *Whack- a-Mole?*)[2]

I gave and I gave, and he took and he took. Occasionally he would throw me a bone or two, a small morsel that tasted of love. I settled for crumbs of affection and attention, as I, too, was hungry.

'*Please, Sir, I want some more.*'[3] (Note: Emotional crumbs do *not* make a meal.)

Speaking of meals, Prince Alpha Wolf remained ravenous. He was insatiable. '*More! More! More!*' was his incessant bark.

I went from sheep-walking to sheep-running, desperate to keep up with his ever-increasing demands. (Remember the over-giver: over-taker ratio?)

Mind you, it wasn't all bad. Narcissists excel at something known as Intermittent Reinforcement. They sprinkle in just enough good stuff to keep you hooked. We love-starved sheep become addicted to these tiny treats, these hints of more to come. Because here's the thing: '*When he was good, he was very, very good.*'

One minor problem: '*But when he was bad, he was* **horrid**.'[4]

What happens when an over-giver meets an over-taker, you ask? It's simple: She is overtaken. And taken over.

Who let the wolf in?

Oops. I did it again.[5]

Lamb Stew: The Boiling Frog and the Sheep Who Finally Cried, "Wolf!"

You've heard the parable of the frog in boiling water?[6]

Emotional abuse is like that. At first you enjoy the warmth of this cozy bath, you feel safe and taken care of. Then oh-so-slowly the heat is turned up and up and up and...

'Mmm... mutton,' murmurs the big, bad wolf in gleeful anticipation of his next mouthful. *'Sleep, little lamb chop, sleep.'*

The sheep sleeps.

'Sleep, stupid sheep, sleep!'

But... the sheep doesn't sleep. This time the frog doesn't croak. There will be no boiled frog, no meal of mutton. For the Me-Wolf has awakened. We all have boiling points, yes?

I simmered and simmered for twenty years in a simmering stew of emotional abuse, until my repressed anger and my festering wounds, old and new, began to bubble to the surface, ready to burst. What was the turning point, my boiling point, you ask? Hmmm...

Well, there was the ever-cliché, *'I love you, but I'm not in love with you.'* (Insert eye roll here.)

Or *'I'm not sure I see myself married forever.'* (Ok, until when then?)

How about this one: *'I always figured if I wasn't happy, I could just get out.'* (Gosh, I missed that memo when we took our vows.)

This one's a classic, given that he knowingly-- and proudly-- married a female doctor: *'I realize I don't necessarily need to be with a smart woman.'* (Uh… ok.)

Along the same lines: *'I realize now, you're a F..F..Feminist!'* (Now he's dropping his version of F-bombs.)

And, who could forget the glare in his eyes as he shoved a clump of dead roses-- with extra thorns-- at me on what was to be our last Valentine's Day? (No card needed; I got the message.)

I sacrificed myself for *this*? I dimmed down, dumbed down, denied, and numbed for *this*?

This would-be wolf woman was now awakened and revived. A bit wobbly, but alive, a-sheep no more.

Ignorance is no longer bliss. Denial is no longer a river in Egypt. Lamb stew is no longer on the menu.

Welcome back, Me-Wolf. You may take the wheel.

(Insert howl here.)

Four Sheeps to the Wind: A Wounded Wolf and Her Wine

Here's the ugly truth: I escaped the pot, but I hit the wall.

The aftermath of a destructive marriage and a grueling divorce is often not pretty. It certainly wasn't in my case. My wounds had surfaced, and they hurt. A lot. Then there were those *wtf* growing pains, which are, not surprisingly, *wtf painful*. I had seen the light, only to fall into a Dark Night of the Soul.[7] If only it were just *a night* and not so many damn nights… The dangers of life with a wicked wolf had been replaced with intractable insomnia. (You mean I have to face these damn dark nights *awake*?)

There's a scene in the Sex and the City movie in which our plucky heroine, Carrie, responds to the shock and devastation of having been jilted at the altar by Mr. Big (another wolf in sheep's clothing, but I digress…) by sleeping. And sleeping. And sleeping. She slept for days. Lucky lady. How I envied Carrie her prolonged slumber!

Here I was, a narrowly boiled sheep, now a wobbly wounded wolf, and I was *awake*. And in pain. So, I attempted to dilute the pain and the loneliness, and give myself the gift of sleep with… sleeping pills. And wine.

Not smart. Not safe. Not pretty. A terribly *bad* choice. I repeatedly embarrassed myself, and I scared and embarrassed my kids and my family. Oh, the shame! (Fuck.)

I had hit the wall. I had had a great fall. It was time to detox, time to recover, time to put myself back together again.

It was time to reclaim my wild, true nature.

Recall of the Wild: The Long and Wilding Road

"If you do not express your own original ideas, if you do not listen to your own being, you will have betrayed yourself."— Rollo May, *The Courage to Create*

I had hit the wall.

What I didn't know: Healing from the drama and trauma of narcissistic abuse takes time, energy, self-compassion, patience, and determination. (And a ton of therapy, loving and loyal community, and lots of she-wolf support.) It was time to find my way back to the woods I once knew. I had to rediscover, reclaim, and reconnect with my truest, wildest self, my Me-Wolf.

But, how?

Carrie Fisher said, *'Take your broken heart, make it into art.'*

I had a broken heart... Who am I not to listen to Carrie Fisher? It was time to make some art.[8] It was time to explore, to express, to create. It was time to howl. It was time to *play*.

Welcome back, Goofiness. Welcome back, Curiosity. Welcome back, Mischief.

Welcome back, my wandering, wondering, wonderful Me-Wolf.

Welcome home, Hermie.

Pack to the Future: Riding in the 'Hood

"Look for the helpers."-- Mister Rogers

None of us is meant to live, love, or heal alone.

It takes a village, as they say.[9] We must seek out our village, our tribe, our guides, our helpers, our pack. We wolves, as you know, travel in packs. The woods can be treacherous and unpredictable. The woods can be dark. I will bring my light. I will bring my love. My Me-Wolf will show up with her intuition, ferocity, vitality, and passion. I am done sitting, staying, rolling over, and playing dead.

Welcome to these wild, wild woods. Welcome to the pack. Welcome to the 'hood.

Let's get packin'-- We ride at dawn!

Epilogue: "Which Wolf Will You Feed?"

There is a story of an old Cherokee and his grandson. The old Cherokee was teaching his grandson about life.

'A fight is going on inside me,' he said to the boy.

'It is a terrible fight, and it is between two wolves. One is evil—he is anger, envy, sorrow, regret, greed, arrogance, self-pity, guilt, resentment, inferiority, lies, false pride, superiority, and ego.'

He continued, *'The other is good—he is joy, peace, love, hope, serenity, humility, kindness, benevolence, empathy, generosity, truth, compassion, and faith. The same fight is going on inside you—and inside every other person, too.'*

The grandson thought about it for a minute and then asked his grandfather: *'Which wolf will win?'*

The grandfather simply replied, *'The one you feed.'*

Final Words: Feeding the Wolf

I sacrificed too many years feeding the wolf spirits of others, attuning and attending to their agendas, and following their scripts in my attempts to win approval and acceptance. In doing so, I neglected and negated my own intuition and instincts. I abandoned my Me-Wolf. My spirit was dampened, my psyche damaged, my soul deadened.

By revisiting and tending to my still-open wounds, rediscovering my passions, reasserting my voice (howls and all), and by resurrecting my creativity and playfulness (Welcome home, wolf pup!), I have brought my life back to life. I have found my ferocity. The *'wolfie in the window'* is no longer window dressing, and no longer for sale.

I urge and encourage you: Walk or run -- or do a frog's leap or limp— out of the pot, out of the penned-in pasture, away from those who would have you boiled alive or remain a sheep asleep.

Find your pack—those fellow travelers who support you, honor you, guide you, follow you—those who will laugh, cry and howl with you.

Heed the call of the wild. Pursue your greatest passions. Drink in your desires and seek out that which is most soul-affirming. Flaunt your irrepressible joys. Fuel them. Explore and express.

Celebrate your finest, fiercest Me-Wolf.

Then, feed her well.

'Aooooooo....!'

Notes

1. Paraphrased line from classic horror movie, "When a Stranger Calls"
2. An arcade game, also a situation in which repeated efforts to resolve a problem are frustrated by the problem reappearing in a different form
3. Charles Dickens, *Oliver Twist*
4. Paraphrased from "The Little Girl with a Curl"— nursery rhyme
5. "Oops!... I Did it Again"—Britney Spears

6. It goes like this: If you place a frog in a pot of boiling water it will immediately jump out. If, however, the water is initially tepid then slowly heated, the frog will boil to death.
7. A stage in personal development during which one undergoes a difficult and significant transition towards a deeper perception of life
8. A huge part of my healing process involved immersing myself in the art of Assemblage. You can see some of my weird and wacky creations on my Instagram or Facebook (@whybebeige) or on my website (www.whybebeige).
9. "It takes a village to raise a child"—African proverb
10. Native American legend often attributed to the Cherokees

ABOUT THE AUTHOR
VALERIE SUSSMAN, MD.

Valerie Sussman, MD. describes herself as, 'A formerly well-behaved pediatrician who plays with toys and words to make weird and wacky healing art.'

She collects, dissects, and combines observations, insights, and seemingly random objects in order to explore, explain, and express life's full spectrum. (In other words, she is trying to make sense of non-sense.)

The back story: At the age of fifty Valerie found herself facing the "Triple Threat." Unfortunately, this did not include Singing, Dancing, and Acting—but that other (perhaps more common) "Triple Threat": Midlife, Menopause, and… Divorce.

Sadly not possessing the skill set of that more desirable three-some, she began maniacally creating somewhat quirky pieces of art as a means of delving into and facing her pain, fear, sadness, and anger… and, yes, even hope.

She thus became a Healing Artist.

Her art is made for anyone who can use some light with their dark—and some laughter with their tears.

This is her work— and this is her play.

Her hope is to heal others as she heals herself.

(Once a doctor, always a doctor...)

You can connect with Valerie online at www.whybebeige.com

instagram.com/whybebeige

Printed in Great Britain
by Amazon